Vice Presidential Profiles

VICE PRESIDENTIAL PROFILES

OUR FORGOTTEN LEADERS

Philip Secor

iUniverse, Inc.
Bloomington

VICE PRESIDENTIAL PROFILES
OUR FORGOTTEN LEADERS

iUniverse books may be ordered through booksellers or by contacting:

iUniverse
1663 Liberty Drive
Bloomington, IN 47403
www.iuniverse.com
1-800-Authors (1-800-288-4677)

ISBN: 978-1-4759-8554-2 (sc)
ISBN: 978-1-4759-8555-9 (e)

Printed in the United States of America.

iUniverse rev. date: 5/3/2013

TABLE OF CONTENTS

FORWARD

W HY WOULD ANYONE WANT to be vice president of the United States? A good question! The vice presidency is, after all, more often than not one of the most insignificant and unimportant of all public positions in the country. The members of the president's cabinet have more real power built into their positions as heads of the leading executive organs of national government. Congressmen in both the House of Representatives and Senate have more influence on American life, as do members of the Supreme Court. One is tempted to include in this list of officials more important than the vice president: governors, state legislators and even the mayors of major cities.

The U.S. Constitution says very little about the vice presidency, stipulating that the office is to be filled by election at the same time and in the same manner and for the same four-year term as the president and that, in the event that for any reason the president should leave office during his term, the vice president shall become president for the remainder of the term (Article II, Section 1). Nine vice presidents have become president in this manner: eight on the death of the president and one when the president resigned his office. The other thirty-three never became president and are thus largely forgotten in our history. Except for stipulating that, like the president, the vice president is subject to impeachment for treason and other "high crimes and misdemeanors" (Article II), the only other important sections stipulate that the vice president shall preside over sessions of the Senate and may cast a vote in case of a deadlock in that body (Article1) and that in the case of a vacancy in the vice presidency, the president may appoint a replacement with the approval of both houses of Congress (25th Amendment).

At the outset of our examination of the lives and careers of each of the vice presidents who never realized their wish to become president, we are tempted to conclude that the most likely explanation for a desire by highly qualified persons to want such an insignificant post is they hope that death or some other ill fate will befall the president and they will simply inherit the post exalted of all political positions in the country. But whatever their motives may have been, one thing is certain. These men were highly accomplished and prominent leaders in public life <u>before</u> they became vice president.

Some commentators have wrongly concluded that because they sought such a powerless post as the vice presidency they must have been in other respects undistinguished and unimportant figures. One such commentator, Tony Horowitz, in the August, 2012 issue of the *Smithsonian*, has gone so far as to suggest that the fact that these men are no longer remembered is owing to the "mediocrity (or worse)of these second stringers" who have often been regarded as "light agents, bench warmers and easy targets of derision." "Bench warmers" while vice presidents, no doubt—but "lightweights"? Absolutely not!

In the pages that follow we will discover some of the most important leaders of our country since the founding of the Republic—men whose service as vice president was usually the least significant part of their contribution to American history whether or not they ever became president. Much of the information is drawn from excellent biographical accounts by noted historians contained in a 1998 book edited by L. Edward Purcell and titled, simply, *Vice Presidents*.

As with my previous books, I am deeply indebted to my wife and friend, Anne Smith Secor, for her keen editorial eye and many helpful suggestions.

AARON BURR
(Library of Congress)

AARON BURR, JR.
(1756-1836)
1801-1805
Infamous Aaron

I

OUR THIRD VICE PRESIDENT—THE first never to become president—was so famous—some would say infamous—that he is better known today than many vice presidents of more recent years. Aaron Burr's very name has been synonymous with "traitor' for most of our history even though, as we shall see, this is probably a false accusation promoted by the man under whom he served as vice president and who virtually hated him with an undying ardor—none other than Thomas Jefferson.

Aaron Burr was born in Newark, New Jersey in 1756, the son of the Rev. Aaron Burr, Sr. who was president of Princeton University (called the College of New Jersey at the time) and Esther Edwards Burr, the daughter of the most famous Protestant theologian of the day, Jonathan Edwards. He was orphaned at the age of two and raised by family and friends. At age thirteen he entered Princeton and received his B.A. degree three years later in 1772.

After college, Burr served for a time in the army during the Revolution. He fought under General Benedict Arnold at the Battle of

Quebec and earned a spot on General Washington's staff. Fighting in many battles he earned a reputation for bravery in the field. However, in 1778 his regiment was defeated at the Battle of Monmouth and he subsequently stepped down as a field commander serving thenceforth as one of Washington's chief intelligence officers.

II

In 1782 Burr opened a law practice in New York City and two years later made his entry into politics. Following a term in the New York Assembly and two years as the state's Attorney General, he was elected in 1791 to the U.S. Senate. He claimed almost at once that he was "bored" in the Senate with nothing of importance to occupy his time. After one term he was appointed by President Adams to be Commanding General of all U.S. military forces. (George Washington, it should be noted, gave voice to the mixed feeling many at the time had about Burr. No doubt, he said, as a military man Burr is "a brave and able officer but the question is whether he has equal talents at intrigue.")

Following a brief return stint in the New York Assembly in 1798, Burr became the leading figure in New York politics, creating and running the largest political machine in the country at the time— Tamany Hall. With the indispensible aid of Burr's machine, Jefferson won election to the presidency in 1800. In the meantime Burr became the de facto head of the new Republican-Democratic Party which created the two-party system as it stood in opposition to the Federalist party led by Alexander Hamilton.

In the presidential election of 1800, Jefferson rewarded Burr by naming him his running mate. But the two men received an equal number of votes in the Electoral College. After thirty-six ballots, Burr encouraged some of his Electors to support Jefferson and took the number two post for himself.

While serving as vice president, Burr rarely enjoyed the support of Jefferson who never really trusted him and gave him very little responsibility in his administration. Burr was, nevertheless, widely admired in the Senate for his fair and judicious manner in presiding over that body. When Jefferson ran for a second term in 1804, he gladly dropped Burr as his running mate. Aaron then ran for governor of New York and lost, partly because of the vicious campaign waged against him by George Clinton and Alexander Hamilton. In one of many personal attacks on his character, Hamilton said that he was "a dangerous man and one who ought not be trusted with the reins of government."

III

Exasperated with Hamilton's repeated attacks over a fifteen year period, Burr finally demanded a public apology. When Hamilton refused to oblige, Burr challenged him to a duel. The two met a Weehawken, New Jersey—a State in which dueling was illegal—on July 11, 1804. Hamilton was mortally wounded and died the next day. There is still dispute among historians as to whether Hamilton designed his gun with a hair-trigger to fire more rapidly. What is not in dispute is that his shot missed and Burr's bullet hit him in the liver and spine. Whatever the details, Jefferson saw to it that Burr was immediately charged with murder. Burr fled to his daughter's home in South Carolina but returned soon thereafter when charges were dropped and completed his term as vice president.

Jefferson did not give up in his dogged determination to destroy Burr. In 1807, he pushed for and got a trial for treason in which Burr was charged for illegal seizure and sale of government land in the west. It was claimed that while siding with Mexico in the Spanish-American War he had leased some 40,000 acres from Spain and now planned to claim it as his own. There was no evidence of this transaction except for a letter which he had allegedly written to the Spanish and British Ambassadors in Washington concerning the transaction. (This incriminating letter was probably forged by one of Burr's Jeffersonian accusers.) In any event, the two witnesses required in any trial for treason under Article 3, Section 3 of the Constitution failed to appear at Burr's trial and so he was acquitted by another of those whom

Jefferson disliked, none other than Chief Justice John Marshall who presided over the trial .

IV

Acquitted or not, Burr's reputation was ruined and he left the country after the trial in 1808, moving at first to France and later to England where he became a close friend to Jeremy Bentham, the already famous Utilitarian philosopher. In 1812, he returned to his law practice in New York City, living there quietly until his death twenty-four years later in 1836 at the age of 80.

Just three years before his death, Burr married, for a second time, to the "fast" and wealthy widow, Eliza Bowen Jumel. She was much too much form him and they divorced within a year. His earlier marriage, in 1792, had been to Theodora Prevost, the widow of a British officer n the Revolution. Only one child survived this marriage. But there are two other children attributed to this irrepressible man. Both were born to his servant Mary Emmonds while he was still married to Theodora.

There can be no doubt that Aaron Burr had a complex personality. On the one hand, he was described by those who knew him as "generous," kind," "honest," "reliable." Others used such terms as "self-interested," "vain," "unpredictable," "ruthless," to describe this amazing person.

What is not in doubt about Burr is that he was an early and ardent supporter of both Black and women's rights. He stated clearly that he believed women to be in all respects equal to men—especially in their mental capacities. As for slavery, he opposed it throughout his career, beginning as early as 1784 when he sought legislation in the New York Assembly to eliminate it.

GEORGE CLINTON
(Library of Congress)

GEORGE CLINTON
(1739-1812)
1805-1812
Negative George

I

SERVING UNDER BOTH THOMAS Jefferson and James Madison, our fourth vice president, like his three predecessors, was one of the most influential public figures in the early history of the Republic. Clinton was the first governor of New York, serving in that office for twenty-two years from 1777 to 1795. While serving as governor, he became one of our "founding fathers" as a delegate to the Constitutional Convention in 1778.

Despite his prominence at the time, Clinton is largely forgotten today. His nephew, DeWitt Clinton, is much better remembered. He was like his uncle, an important public figure, serving as mayor of New York City, governor of the New York and member of the U.S. Senate. He was also a candidate for the presidency in 1812, carrying most all of the northern states against Madison. But what makes DeWitt so well remembered is none of these accomplishments. What made his lasting reputation is that he was the leading force behind the building of the Erie Canal which opened in 1825.

George Clinton was of Scotch-Irish heritage. His parents were Presbyterians (Calvinists) who had fled Ireland in 1729 and come to America to escape the Anglican regime there. His father, Charles Clinton, was a prosperous and well-connected farmer and land speculator in the New York City area by the time of George's birth in 1739.

Until the age of eighteen, George was tutored by a Scottish clergyman but never received a formal education. As a result he was only partially literate for his entire life—never really able to write coherently.

After serving for two years in the colonial army during the French and Indian War, Clinton read law in New York City under renowned attorney William Smith and began his own legal practice in 1764. He also continued in his father's career as a land speculator and was a very wealthy man by the time he entered politics in 1768 by election to the New York Assembly.

During the years up to the Revolution, Clinton, although as always a modest and assuming person, assumed something of a leadership role among politicians opposing British rule. Along with the Livingstons, who were the most powerful family in New York at the time, he became a leader in *The Sons of Liberty*, a powerful revolutionary group. In 1775, Clinton was elected to the Second Continental Congress and soon thereafter was made a Brigadier General in the New York Militia. He was heroic during several successful battles fought along the Hudson River Valley which prevented the British from controlling that vital river artery.

II

While the war still raged, Clinton was elected the first governor of New York in 1777 in an upset victory over the powerful Livingston family with whom he had previously been allied. He was supported by the very farmers and "common folk" who had benefited from his victories as an army general in the farm country along the Hudson River. Soon he was the most dominant figure in New York public life.

As governor, Clinton vigorously opposed the ever-increasing power of the national government over the states, especially the imposition of tariffs and the creation of a national bank. He advocated what he regarded as a true federal system in which the states were the locus of power and in so doing became a leading foe of Alexander Hamilton.

As a delegate to the Constitutional Convention in 1788, Clinton tried to unite opponents of the new constitution but failing in this effort he reluctantly voted for its adoption. In this same year he ran against John Adams for the vice presidency and lost in that effort as well—overwhelmingly. (In those days, before adoption of the Twelfth Amendment to the Constitution in 1804, the candidate with the second largest vote in the presidential election automatically became vice president.) In 1792 he ran again and lost to Adams a second time but the vote was much closer: 77-50.

III

Following a brief retirement from public life, Clinton ran successfully for the New York State legislature in 1795. Six years later he resigned this position to run for the governorship and won overwhelmingly. Then, in 1805, he finally achieved his long desire for national office when Jefferson selected him to replace Aaron Burr as his running mate for the presidency. Clinton was sixty-two years old and in ill health at the time and this is probably why Jefferson chose him as his running mate. Clearly, he would be no threat to run in 1808 against Jefferson's favorite, James Madison.

Much to Jefferson's chagrin, Clinton did run in 1808 and became Madison's vice president. To demonstrate his utter dislike of Clinton, the new president almost totally ignored him and never—so far as we can tell—sought his advice. Clinton was rarely even invited to attend cabinet meetings. Nevertheless, he was very popular in the social life of Washington.

The vice president was not so popular, however in his conduct as presiding officer of the Senate. He often did not attend meetings at all and when he did seemed distracted and ineffectual. Senator Plummer said of him that he had a "clumsy, awkward manner" and "preserved little of no order."

Throughout his term, Clinton worked against all of Madison's programs, most notably casting a deciding vote in the Senate against the president's bill to charter a national bank. (So intense was the dislike of the two men for one another that Clinton had not even attended Madison's inauguration as president.)

IV

On August 20, 1812, while still serving as vice president, George Clinton died and was the first person ever to lie in state in the Capitol building.

ELBRIDGE GERRY
(Library of Congress)

ELBRIDGE GERRY
(1744-1814)
1813-1814
Gerrymander Gerry

I

ONE OF THE LEAST remembered but most important men in early nineteenth century America was our fifth vice president, Elbridge Gerry. A "founding father" in every sense of the word, Gerry was a signer of the Declaration of Independence, a member of the Continental Congress, a war hero, a delegate to the Constitutional Convention, a member of the first U.S. Congress, ambassador to France and governor of Massachusetts.

Despite these accomplishments, about the only thing for which Gerry is remembered, if at all, is lending his name to a notorious process for fixing election districts to favor the party in power—a process called "gerry-mandering." But more of that later.

Elbridge Gerry was born in 1744, the third of twelve children, in the prosperous port city of Marblehead, Massachusetts. His father, Thomas, was one of the leading merchants in the area who became very wealthy in trade with England. So prominent and financially secure was Thomas that there was no doubt that his children would have every advantage he could provide. For his part, Elbridge not only attended Harvard, where he earned his BA and MA degrees, but he also followed in his father's path by becoming wealthy in the merchant trading business. At the same time, his pleasant and out-going manner secured him a place among the city's most popular personalities.

II

In 1773, not yet thirty years old, Gerry entered politics and was elected easily to the General Court of Massachusetts (the colonial legislature) where he immediately assumed the role of a strong advocate for separation from England—with the proviso that state militia and not an enlarged federal army should fight the inevitable war for independence. This was the first of a life- time of promoting states' rights over a growing national government and insisting that "federal" meant government by popularly elected state governments with very little independent power for the central government—an attitude much the same as that of his predecessor, George Clinton.

Early in the Revolution, Gerry became something of a war hero during the historic battles at Lexington and Concord in April, 1775. At the time, he chaired a state committee responsible for weapons stored at Concord which the British badly wanted to seize. During the enemy attack, Gerry and his committee colleagues, who were guarding the weapons, managed to escape in their pajamas and hide in a nearby cornfield.

The following year, Gerry, now a Massachusetts delegate to the Continental Congress, signed the Declaration of Independence and became a strong advocate of all-out war with Britain. However, once the war was over he reverted to his earlier opposition to a national army and insisted on a return to state militias as the sole military forces in the new nation. Continuing his service in the Continental Congress until 1793, Gerry opposed almost every effort to strengthen the central government, including the introduction of national tariffs.

Meantime, in 1786, Elbridge met and married the love of his life, the beautiful and sophisticated Ann Thompson. She was a member of a prominent family in New York City and twenty-one years his junior. Under her influence he soon became a polished gentleman, conservative and very polite in his social manner. He also ended his long-time anti-English attitudes and even joined the Anglican Church.

Shortly after his marriage, Gerry was elected as a delegate from Massachusetts to the U.S. Constitutional Convention. He voted against adoption of the Constitution not only on the general grounds that it created what he regarded as far too strong a central government but, more specifically, because it lacked a Bill of Rights (later adopted) and allowed for a general popular election of the president rather than election by states. Most importantly—and ironically—Gerry opposed the Constitution because of the only specific power it gave to the vice president, namely to preside over the Senate. This power, he argued, was a violation of the principle of separation of powers, because it would allow the president, in effect, to control Congress.

Once the Constitution was ratified in 1789, Gerry changed his position and supported it. In that same year he became a member of Congress and a strong supporter of Hamilton and the Federalist Party during the presidency of John Quincy Adams. In 1797, Adams appointed Gerry as part of a delegation to negotiate with France over that country's interference with U.S. shipping by stopping our ships at sea, "impressing" sailors and seizing goods from the ships. The three American delegates met with three unnamed French negotiators called "X," "Y," and "Z." When Marshall and Pinckney returned home because France had demanded a huge financial payment for avoiding war with them, Elbridge remained and was refused a passport to leave the country and return home. Gerry was blamed for accepting the hated French offer in what came to be known as the "XYZ Affair." John Marshall went so far as to brand him a "traitor."

By 1800, Gerry had returned to Massachusetts and run successfully for governor of the state. He tried again in three succeeding elections and lost them all. Finally, in 1810 he was elected governor and re-elected in 1812. It was during this latter election that the term "gerrymandering" was first used. It seems that as the sitting governor, Gerry had used his power to get a bill through the legislature to redraw election district lines in such as way as to guarantee his re-election.

III

Gerry never really served his last term as governor because President John Quincy Adams chose him as his running mate in 1812. Of course, this meant that Gerry had to abandon his membership in the Federalist Party and join the Democratic- Republican Party, something he was apparently all too willing to do if it meant he might become vice president. By this time, Gerry was in poor health and sixty-eight years old.

As vice president, Gerry, like Clinton before him, had little work to do. Unlike his predecessor, however, he took seriously his duties as presiding officer of the Senate, attending meetings regularly and officiating with appropriate decorum. Also, like Clinton—and despite his age and poor health—he managed to cut a lively figure in Washington social life.

In November of 1814, after less than two years as vice president, Gerry died of a stroke after about a year's illness at aged seventy. He is little remembered today save for two towns in Massachusetts named in his honor, "Elbridge" and "Gerry" and the notorious practice of "gerrymandering."

DANIEL D. TOMPKINS
(Library of Congress)

DANIEL TOMPKINS
(1774-1825)
1817-1825
Drunken Dan

I

DANIEL TOMPKINS WAS THE third successive of our "forgotten" vice presidents. He was less antagonistic toward the president under whom he served than they were but was nevertheless a terrible embarrassment to President Monroe because of his drunken behavior and use of foul language, directed sometimes at him—and in public.

Like the other vice presidents during these early years of the Republic, Tompkins was a highly respected and long-serving governor—in his case of New York. Like them, he was also very active during a major war in the early years of the Republic—in his case the War of 1812. For his leadership in this war he became something of a folk hero known affectionately as "the farmer's boy."

Tompkins was born in Scarsdale, New York (Westchester County) in 1774. His father, Jonathan, was a prosperous and poplar farmer who was successful in local and state politics assuring Daniel the advantages of an affluent and well-connected career as he set out on his own to attend Columbia College, graduating with a pre-law degree as class valedictorian in 1795. Soon after college, he was admitted to the New

York bar and began his legal practice in New York City. At about this time, he married Hannah Menthorne whose family was prominent in city politics and business. Although Hannah was sick for most of their marriage, the couple had eight children. (She was too ill even to attend his inauguration as vice president in 1817.)

II

Tomkins began his political career in earnest at the age of twenty-seven, shortly after his marriage, when he was chosen as a delegate to the New York State Constitutional Convention. In 1804, he was elected to the New York State Assembly but resigned almost at once when he was chosen to be an associate justice of the New York Supreme Court. He left this post as well after only three years in 1807 and ran successfully for Governor of New York for the first of five terms ending in 1817.

By the time Tomkins became governor, he was already an ardent political foe of the most powerful family in state politics: the Clintons. As governor, he went so far as to try to remove DeWitt Clinton as mayor of New York City, a post to which his uncle, former governor George Clinton, had appointed him. Tompkins rarely missed an opportunity to disparage and discredit DeWitt, especially regarding the latter's major project—the building of the Erie Canal.

As governor of New York during the War of 1812, Tomkins was especially effective in organizing the state militia to fight the British, going so far as to invest his own money to pay salaries and purchase arms and other needed supplies. By the time the war ended, he was in dire financial straits due to his generous support of the militia. The federal government had promised to reimburse him some $90,000 (a virtual fortune in those days) but they never did. This left him financially bereft, increasingly depressed and, finally, to excessive use of alcohol.

III

By 1816, Tomkins was nationally known and respected for his outstanding work as governor of New York, who had been a leader in the 1812 War effort, as well as for his record as an advocate of education and welfare for the poor, especially Black Americans. He decided to make a run for the presidency against James Monroe. The two had the same number of electoral votes and so, under the Constitutional provisions of the day, Congress made the final choice and selected Monroe as president and Tomkins automatically was awarded the number two post and became vice president.

By this time his excessive drinking had become a serious issue. He appeared drunk on many public occasions, including those few times when he even bothered to accept his vice presidential responsibility to preside over sessions of the Senate. Apparently sober enough to be elected to a second term as vice president under Monroe, he soon reverted to his drunken behavior turning the vice presidential office into a debacle.

IV

In 1825, only ninety-nine days after leaving office, Tomkins died. He had had the shortest life after serving as vice president of any who survived the office. He is buried in the family vault in St. Mark's Churchyard in Manhattan. His wife, Hannah, joined him there four years later.

As one of most completely forgotten vice presidents, Daniel Tomkins has not many lasting memorials—only a few parks, roads, schools and small towns named for him in his native New York.

JOHN CALDWELL CALHOUN
(Library of Congress)

JOHN C. CALHOUN
(1782-1850)
1825-1832
Nullification John

I

JOHN C. CALHOUN IS probably better remembered today than his four predecessor vice presidents especially in the southeastern part of the country, which is the home of the old States of the Confederacy. He is remembered there fondly by many as the founding spirit of the secessionist movement that led to the Civil War.

The first vice president from the South since Thomas Jefferson in 1797, Calhoun was the son of a prosperous plantation owner of Scotch-Irish background. Not surprisingly, John was raised in a strict Calvinist Presbyterian household where discipline, hard work and personal integrity were the order of the day. He was born on March 18, 1782 in a small and remote settlement near Abbeville, South Carolina in the northwestern part of the state close to the Savannah River and the border with Georgia. (Today's Calhoun Falls, on the river, probably marks a place close to where he was born.)

In 1804, at age twenty-two, Calhoun received his undergraduate degree with Phi Beta Kappa honors from Yale University in far away New Haven Connecticut. Remaining in the north for another three years, the promising young man studied law at Tapping Reeve Law School, also in Connecticut, and then returned to his native South Carolina to be admitted to the bar and begin law practice.

II

Shortly before beginning his legal career, Calhoun was elected to the South Carolina House of Representatives in 1808. Just two years later, he was elected to the U. S. House of Representatives and became one of the major leaders in Congress as one of what soon was called "The Great Triumvirate": Daniel Webster, Henry Clay and John C. Calhoun. In Congress he was known as a "war hawk," a Congressman vehemently opposed to the pending British invasion of the country which would shortly lead to the War of 1812. Early in his career in Congress, he was hailed as a great national leader. John Quincy Adams said of him in his diary in 1821:

> Calhoun is a man of fair and candid mind, of honorable principles, of clear and quick understanding, of cool self-understanding, of enlarged philosophical views and of ardent patriotism. He is above all sectional and factional prejudices more than any other statesman with whom I have interacted

As we shall see, it was not many years before Adams radically altered this favorable assessment of Calhoun.

Meanwhile, while serving in Congress, John married his cousin, Floride Calhoun in 1811. The couple had ten children, seven of whom survived infancy. Floride was an Episcopalian with little use for Presbyterians. For his part, John had never been much interested in religion and had largely abandoned church attendance once he left home. Like Thomas Jefferson, he was probably a Unitarian, though he never formally joined any church.

In 1817, President James Monroe appointed Calhoun Secretary of War. He held this post for both of Monroe's terms in the White House until 1825. As Secretary of War, he provided personal financial support for the arming of the troops of an expanding army, led efforts to improve the management of military forces and, after the war, pushed for a strong national standing army.

He also was instrumental in creating the Bureau of Indian Affairs as a branch of the War Department and personally negotiated dozens of treaties with Native American tribes. As part of his growing efforts to strengthen the national government *viz a viz* the states, he also pressed for national tariffs, a national bank and internal improvements including roads, seaports and canals.

III

In 1824, John Quincy Adams and Andrew Jackson were the rival candidates for the presidency. Calhoun ran for the vice presidency and was elected overwhelmingly in the Electoral College. He had supported Jackson for the presidency but when neither he nor Adams gained a majority in the Electoral College, the House of Representative selected Adams as the next president. As vice president, Calhoun opposed Adams on many policies because he saw them as too nationalistic and thus a threat to the power of the states to govern their own affairs. The two men came to hate each other.

Calhoun justified his opposition to the so-called "Tariff of Abominations" in terms of what he termed the doctrine of "nullification" under which a state had the right to stop the application of any federal law within its jurisdiction if it regarded that law as unconstitutional. At about the same time, he also put forth his theory of a "concurrent majority" according to which a minority could, under certain circumstances, block the application of what it regarded as a bad federal law.

After being elected to a second term as vice president in 1828, this time on Andrew Jackson's ticket, Calhoun continued his strong States-rights emphases but this time under a very nationalist president. He became the author, for example, of the so-called "Calhoun Doctrine" which asserted that the federal government had no authority to prohibit slavery in the territories because only the states had such power. All of these positions: "concurrent majority," "nullification," and the "Calhoun doctrine," were perceived by Jackson as a threat by his own vice president to his advocacy of growing national power.

(Calhoun's strongly held and widely known political ideas and policies were expressed for posterity in several significant works. Important among these are: *A Disquisition on Government* and *Discourse on the Constitution and Government of the United States*, both of which were published after his death in 1850 and established his reputation as an important American political theorist.)

In 1832, Jackson's Congress passed the *Force Bill*, which gave the president the power to use the military to force obedience to federal law. Jackson then sent the navy to enforce a tariff law. In the midst of the ensuing opposition of Calhoun, the president threatened to have him hanged as a traitor. Before long, a compromise tariff bill was developed which Calhoun reluctantly accepted.

Another significant event toward the end of Calhoun's vice presidency under Jackson would probably have ended his once cordial relationship with the president if all of the aforementioned events had not even occurred. This was the so-called "petticoat affair" which involved Secretary of War John Eaton's wife, Peggy. Calhoun's wife, Floride, led fellow cabinet wives in personal attacks on Peggy's character and Jackson felt that Calhoun was behind all this simply to sow dissention in the cabinet and hurt his presidency. After this, Calhoun's influence within the administration ended altogether.

Following his tumultuous two terms as vice president under two different presidents, Calhoun was appointed Secretary of State by President John Tyler shortly after Tyler inherited the presidency from William Henry Harrison who had died of pneumonia after only a month in office in 1841. By the middle of the decade, Calhoun was well into one of the most successful parts of his long career in public life. As Secretary of State, he was instrumental in acquiring the vast Oregon Territory from Britain. He also presided over and had a major hand in the annexation of Texas (a slave State) to the Union in 1846. This latter action led directly to war with Mexico.

IV

Although Calhoun did not live long enough to be involved in the politics immediately preceding the Civil War of the 1860's, he is usually credited, especially in the South, with being the true author of secession from the Union and the formation of the Confederate States of America which led to the Civil War. Especially were his theories of "concurrent majority" and "nullification" and his actions in behalf of these ideas seen as a rationale for creating a separate nation for the slave-holding states in the South.

Calhoun died in March of 1850 following a long struggle with tuberculosis. At the time, he was widely recognized, not only in the South, as the true author of secession and the Civil War. Among the lasting testimonials to his legacy are Lake Calhoun in Minnesota, Calhoun Hall, a student residence hall and a large statue of him, both at Yale University and many other statues schools, and streets named for him, especially in the South. The U.S. Senate, in 1957, voted him one of the "five greatest Senators of all time." Believe it not, a nuclear submarine named the *John C. Calhoun* was launched in 1963.

Clearly, here was a person whose role as vice president was but a minor episode in an amazing career as political leader and political theorist whose actions and ideas precipitated one of the major defining events of American history.

RICHARD MENTOR JOHNSON
(Library of Congress)

RICHARD JOHNSON
(1780-1850)
1837-1841
Notorious Richard

I

AMONG VICE- PRESIDENTS WHO were well known in their day but are no longer remembered, Richard Mentor Johnson who served in that post from 1737 to 1841 was especially famous—even notorious—during his public career.

Johnson was a colorful figure, to say the least. He was born and raised on the Kentucky frontier, a fierce "Indian" fighter—some say the killer of the great Indian chief, Tecumseh. He was also the founder of many colleges and the perpetrator of what is probably the most scandalous act of any of his fellow vice presidents.

Born in 1780 in a remote settlement in what would become northwestern Kentucky, Johnson's parents were, like many frontier settlers, very much involved both in the battles against the British during the American Revolution and in subsequent vicious efforts to displace Native Americans from their settlements—often by slaughtering them. His father was prominent in the political life of Kentucky, a well-known "Indian fighter" and a member of the legislature who helped draft the first constitution of the new state.

Richard's mother, Jemima, was regarded as one of the few heroines of the Revolution for her brave actions during a British attack on an American fort. The inhabitants had run out of water but were afraid to draw it from a nearby well that was surrounded by Native Americans. At the risk of her own life and that of the few women who accompanied her, Jemima led a run to the well and a safe return to the fort with water. The Native Americans then attacked the fort and proceeded to burn it and its surrounding homes. In one of these houses slept the infant Richard Johnson who would have burned to death had not his mother returned home in time to extinguish the flames with water from the well.

Jemima was a deeply devoted Baptist who unwittingly became a proximate cause of the biggest scandal in Richard's life. It seems that, as a young man still living at home, he fell in love with an older woman and wished to marry her. Jemima responded to this with a firm "No!" The woman, she told her son, is simply not worthy of you or of our family. Richard never forgave his mother for this act and determined to find some way to repay her. Some years later his father died and bequeathed him his slave girl, Julia Chin. Richard informed his mother that he would marry Julia. So there!

According to state law at the time, a white man was forbidden to marry a black woman. No matter. Richard took Julia as his common law wife and lived intimately with her. The couple had two daughters who later married white men! When Julia died in 1833, Richard married another slave woman.

II

Richard was never well educated. In fact he was barely literate for most of his adult life. He may have attended Transylvania College in Lexington, Kentucky for a short time, though there are no records of this. Most historians doubt that he spent any significant time there. After some part- time tutoring in Kentucky law, he was admitted to the bar in 1802 and shortly thereafter was elected to the state legislature.

Between 1807 and 1819 Johnson was a member of the U.S. House of Representatives. As one of the so-called "War Hawks," he raised his own troop of some three-hundred men and fought at the famous Battle of the Thames where he was wounded and credited by some with having personally killed the famous Indian chief, Tecumseh. Although there is much doubt about this claim by many historians, Congress awarded him a ceremonial sword for his valor during the war. Some years later, when he ran for the vice presidency, his campaign slogan was "Rumsey, Dumsey, Rumsey Dumsey, Colonel Johnson killed Tecumsee."

In 1819, the Kentucky legislature sent Johnson as its representative to the U.S. Senate where he served for ten years. While in the Senate, he was especially active in the foundation and support of all levels and types of education. Most notably, he was an advocate for the improvement of life for Native Americans, the very people he had been fighting so viciously just a few years earlier. In 1825, he was the principal founder of the Choctaw Academy, a school for Native Americans. While in the Senate, he was also a leading spirit in the founding of Columbia College (later George Washington University) in Washington D.C. This strong interest in education for all Americans at all levels continued throughout his life.

III

Following his career in the Senate, Johnson served four terms in the House of Representatives before running for the vice presidency on Martin Van Buren's ticket in 1836. He was Andrew Jackson's personal choice to run with his favorite, Van Buren. Jackson, in those days, decided all such matters in the Democratic Party. The primary reason for his choice of Johnson was that he needed a southerner to attract votes from that region of the country as an addition Van Buren's appeal in the north.

However, Johnson failed to get the majority vote required in the Electoral College and so the choice was left to the Senate where he won handily and predictably by a vote of thirty-three to sixteen—strictly along party lines.

Like most vice presidents, Johnson didn't much like the job. His behavior in office often showed his near total disinterest and boredom. Some reported at the time that he was inefficient and sloppy— strolling aimlessly around the Senate when he should have been up front presiding over sessions instead of sitting on the floor, not paying attention and so on. He did, however, cast fourteen tie-breaking votes, one of the highest numbers of any vice president in history.

While vice president, Johnson usually supported Van Buren, mostly because he agreed with the president's moderate approach to all policy issues: better to compromise and perhaps completely satisfy no one than to insist on some viewpoint in the risk alienating a significant portion of the electorate. Gradually, the antagonism which had for so long characterized the relationship between the two men mellowed, although they never became friends.

IV

In retirement, Johnson was active in Kentucky politics. He served in the state House of Representatives from 1841 to 1843 and again in 1850, after an unsuccessful bid for a seat there in 1848. During these years he continued his lively interest in promoting educational opportunities for all Americans. In addition to his ongoing concern for the education of Native Americans, he became active in the creation of military colleges throughout the country.

At the time of his unsuccessful run for reelection with Van Buren in 1840, the Louisville newspaper commented on his frail health both physically and mentally. Especially noteworthy, it was reported, was his incapacity because of an ever worsening dementia.

Returning to Kentucky, John won a seat in the state legislature. He died within two weeks at the age of seventy-nine. There is very little by way of lasting memorials to this remarkable man except for five counties named for him in five different states—one of them in Nebraska!

GEORGE MIFFLIN DALLAS
(Library of Congress)

George M. Dallas
(1792-1864)
1845-1849
Ambassador George

I

YET ANOTHER OF OUR long-forgotten vice presidents is George Dallas who served under James Knox Polk from 1845 to 1849. Like preceding vice-presidents, he was a prominent and widely experienced public figure serving at local, state and national levels of government. Also like his predecessors, he had strong aspirations for the presidency—but, like most of them, he never made it.

II

George Dallas was born in 1792 into a prosperous and politically important Pennsylvania family. He was raised in the Philadelphia area in his family's two homes—a downtown mansion and a luxurious villa on the Schuylkill River—enjoying all of the advantages of wealth. His father, Alexander, a successful attorney, was prominent in Pennsylvania politics and courted for high public office by U.S. presidents beginning with James Madison who appointed him a member of his cabinet, first as Secretary of State and later Secretary of War.

George attended Quaker preparatory schools in the Philadelphia area before entering the College of New Jersey (Princeton University) where he graduated in 1810 as class valedictorian. Several years later, in 1813, the twenty-one year old Dallas travelled to Russia as private secretary to a family friend, Albert Gallatin, who had earlier served as Governor of Pennsylvania and later as Secretary of the Treasury under both Thomas Jefferson and James Madison. Gallatin was on a mission to Russia to gain help from the Tsar in negotiating a treaty to settle international shipping disputes. Although Gallatin was not successful in his mission the trip did give Dallas the opportunity to gain some experience in international affairs traveling further in Europe, visiting prominent leaders not only in Russia but also in Britain and the Netherlands.

As soon as he returned home from his European travels in late 1814, Dallas took a post in the U.S Treasury Department but soon found this work unchallenging and returned to private life in Philadelphia. A more satisfying activity then engaged him for several years as he labored vigorously and successfully to resolve continuing conflicts with Native American tribes over territorial rights. He was finally able to negotiate a treaty with the powerful Indian leader, Tecumseh.

In 1817, during another brief hiatus from public life, Dallas married Sophia Chew Nicklin, the wealthy daughter of a successful Philadelphia businessman. They were to enjoy a happy marriage for nearly fifty years, including eight children.

III

Returning to public life shortly after his marriage, Dallas created what would soon become a powerful political force throughout Pennsylvania. He called his creation "The Family Party." It was a group composed of conservative political and business leaders who favored a very strong national government viz a viz State governments. Specifically, the Family Party pressed for the creation of a national bank, high protective tariffs and extensive internal improvements in roads, bridges, rivers, canals, etc. The Party was influential in promoting, unsuccessfully, the election of John C. Calhoun as President in 1824.

In 1828 Dallas was elected Mayor of Philadelphia. Becoming quickly bored with the job, he resigned within a year and accepted appointment as District Attorney for Eastern Pennsylvania. He and his Family Party supported Andrew Jackson over John Quincy Adams in the election of 1828 despite the fact that Jackson, unlike Dallas' earlier favorite, John C. Calhoun, was the idol of the working class "common man" while Dallas remained a member of the wealthy, conservative business elite. Ever the political opportunist, he was not much bothered by such details.

Soon, however, he became disillusioned with what he came to regard as the "radicalism" of Jackson. By this time, Dallas had been elected a U. S. Senator and had to deal at close hand with policies which he regarded as a direct attack on his nationalist, conservative views. Especially alarming was Jackson's states'-rights approach to virtually all issues. Only two years into his term in the Senate, Dallas resigned and returned to Pennsylvania where he served as attorney general. In this post he fought for penal reform and became something of an advocate for the rights of prisoners, revealing yet another aspect of his often unpredictable political persona.

After three years as State Attorney General, Dallas accepted President Martin Van Buren's appointment as minister to Russia, a position he held for only two years until 1839 before resigning that post because he was largely ignored at the court of the Tsar. (He was, after all, only the representative of a weak, second-class power.)

For the next five years Dallas stayed largely out of public life, limiting himself to a growing law practice. He held no offices and lost most of his former influence in Pennsylvania politics. The new man on the scene, who was growing increasingly powerful in the State, was Senator James Buchanan—himself an aspirant to the position that Dallas most coveted: nothing less that the presidency of the United States.

In the election on 1844, Dallas returned to the political scene and accelerated his aspiration for the presidency by becoming the vice presidential running- mate on James Polk's ticket. Unfortunately for Dallas, Polk, once elected, named Dallas' rival, Buchanan, Secretary of State. The two men became fierce rivals in the Polk administration viewing the president's favor as the surest road to the White House. Dallas eventually won this competition and gained Polk's approval and attention, mostly because of his strong support for the president on the most divisive political issue of the day, tariffs. Polk pushed hard to reduce tariffs because he saw this as crucial to economic recovery in the country. Although Dallas's support of Buchanan on this issue cost him the support of Pennsylvania Democrats, he gained support of southern and western Democrats who also wanted reduced tariffs. Yet another political trade-off aimed at achieving his highest ambition.

A major activity of Dallas during these years was work on behalf of western expansion of the United States. He was a leading spokesman for what was called "manifest destiny"—the inevitable right of the United states to extend its borders across the continent to the Pacific Ocean and also southward to the Caribbean islands and the Mexican border and northward to the Canadian border. If this meant war with Spain, Mexico or even Britain, so be it.

Related to the western expansion issue was the increasingly contentious question of whether slavery should be permitted in the new territories. When Zachary Taylor became president in 1848 and Dallas became a "lame-duck" vice president, he worked hard to persuade Congress to reject the so-called "Wilmot Proviso" which would prevent slavery in all new western lands. He believed that the Constitution guaranteed that each new territory had the right to allow slavery—and he was probably right in this assertion.

IV

After seven years of staying out of the public eye as he pursued his law practice (1849-1856), Dallas accepted President Franklin Pierce's appointment as Minister to Britain. He held this post until 1861 having only limited success in his efforts to limit Britain's growing power in Central America.

Returning to his law practice, Dallas grew increasingly ill and died of a heart attack four years later, in December, 1864. He was seventy-three. One of the least remembered of our vice presidents, one imagines that people living today in the counties and towns named for him in eight different States wonder why they are so-named.

WILLIAM RUFUS DE VANE KING
(Library of Congress)

WILLIAM RUFUS KING
(1786-1853)
1853
Short-Term Rufus

I

ONE IS ALWAYS RELUCTANT to call anyone "unique." But if that characterization applies to any of our vice presidents it would surely be William Rufus King—the thirteenth occupant of that office who, you note, even had the distinction of being number 13!

Among the singular aspects of King's vice presidency are that he served for only twenty-five days in office—by far the shortest term for any vice- president, was the only vice president to be inaugurated outside the country and was, so far as we know, the only homosexual vice president.

Like many vice presidents, King was born into a wealthy and politically important family. His father owned large plantations in North Carolina and Tennessee at the time of William's birth in North Carolina in 1786. While managing his estates, with the help of more than thirty slaves, his father found time to serve as a justice of the peace and member of the North Carolina legislature. His most significant public service was as a delegate to the U. S. Constitutional Convention in Philadelphia in 1787.

As a child, William attended local preparatory schools before entering the University of North /Carolina in 1801. At the end of his junior year, he left the university and began to study law under tutors before opening his own practice in Clinton, North Carolina in 1805.

II

King's political career began when at the age of twenty-two he was elected to the North Carolina legislature as a Jeffersonian-Republican. Two years later, in 1810, he was elected to Congress for the first of three terms. While in the House of Representatives, King was a strong supporter of President James Madison's nationalistic policies, especially regarding the two major issues of the day: high tariffs to support emerging industries and the ending of all British territorial ambitions in North America even if this led to war—which it did in what we know as "The War of 1812." During this fateful conflict, King was one of the leading advocates in the nation of driving the British entirely out of all territory from the Mexican to the Canadian borders and from the Atlantic to the Pacific Oceans.

In 1816, King resigned his seat in Congress to become secretary to William Pinckney, the U.S. Minister to Italy and Russia. In this post he traveled extensively thorough most of Europe meeting the leaders of a number of countries and developing a taste for international diplomacy. Thenceforth, he would believe himself competent to speak out on foreign policy issues and to advise U.S. presidents on what he regarded as the best response to challenges from abroad.

Returning to his home in North Carolina, King soon moved to the new territory of Alabama in 1817 and developed a plantation served by one of largest slave forces in the country. Here he built what was to be his permanent home, an extensive estate which he called "Chestnut Hill." Before long, he was one of the leading figures in the new territory and easily won election to its constitutional convention in 1819—playing the leading role in drafting the state's constitution. Not surprisingly, he was elected as one of the first U.S. Senators from the new State of Alabama. He was to serve in the Senate for four terms, until 1844.

During his long tenure in the Senate, King continued to support tariffs but on a number of other key issues he abandoned his earlier nationalistic positions. For example, he became a strong supporter of state's rights while serving under Andrew Jackson from 1828-1836. He was against establishment of the national bank and strongly opposed "nullification," a policy which would have forbidden slavery in the new territories.

III

In 1852 King ran successfully for the vice presidency on Franklin Pierce's ticket. He had finally achieved his ambition to reach the office which he thought provided the most likely road to the presidency. Almost at once, however, he became seriously ill with tuberculosis (known then as "consumption"). Under his doctor's advice, he went immediately to Cuba to recover his health in a more congenial climate. Unfortunately, his condition only continued to worsen.

When the time came for King's inauguration with Pierce, he was unable to attend. Congress then passed a special act allowing him to be sworn in while still in Havana. That occurred on March 24, 1853 which marks the official beginning of the shortest vice presidential term in history.

IV

In the days immediately following his inauguration, King's health rapidly deteriorated. He was determined to return to his home in Alabama. On April 7, 1853, his 67th birthday, his ship left Havana for Mobile and he finally arrived home at Chestnut Hill on April 17th. He died the next day. He had been vice president for only twenty-five days and spent exactly NONE of that time in Washington performing the duties of his office.

Before ending this account of King's life and career, I would be remiss if I failed to give some account of the most talked about and long remembered aspect of his life which has tended to overshadow his many accomplishments. I refer to his long and intimate relationship with James Buchanan.

While the two men were in Congress, they shared a house near the Capitol in downtown Washington. Buchanan had long been suspected of being gay and now seemed to regard King as his lover. Andrew Jackson called King "Aunt Fancy" and others of the day referred to the pair as "man and wife." Among his frequently noted physical and social attributes were what were seen as his perfect manners and handsome features. He was described at the time as "tall and erect in figure," "well proportioned," of "courtly manners," a true Southern gentleman." He was also referred to as "Mrs. B" and "Buchanan's wife." One commentator went so far as to call him "Aunt Nancy" and to say that "he may be seen everywhere in **her** best clothes and smirking about in hopes of securing better terms with **her** former companion."

Relatives of the pair sought to destroy their letters to one another but one from Buchanan to King has survived. In it, Buchanan says that he was so lonely for King—who was in Europe at the time—that he was "wooing other men." Thus, while there is no eyewitness account of intimate relations, the best circumstantial case is that Buchanan, who was later to be our only homosexual president, had King as his lover—yet one more illustration of the "unique" character of our thirteenth vice president who was in so many other respects one of the most important and accomplished American political figures of the mid-nineteenth century

JOHN CABELL BRECKINRIDGE
(Library of Congress)

JOHN C. BRECKINRIDGE
(1821-1875)
1857-1861
Confederate John

I

ONE OF THE MOST effective and sought-after public speakers in our history was the fourteenth vice president, John Breckinridge of Kentucky. So popular was he as an orator that it would be no exaggeration to say that his entire career, including his run for the presidency against Abraham Lincoln in 1860, was due in large measure to his amazing ability to move people by his speeches.

Among other notable facts about Breckinridge is that he was the youngest vice president, barely making the minimum age of thirty-five required by the Constitution. More importantly, he has the distinction of being a leader in the Southern secessionist movement who was about to be named commander of the Confederate Army while he was still serving as vice president in 1861.

II

John Breckinridge was born in 1821 just outside Lexington, Kentucky. His father died when John was only two years old leaving no inheritance and a large debt. He was raised for a time by his mother, a very stern woman, and later by his older sister and her husband, a prominent Presbyterian minister.

Presbyterian influences were to become very important in John's life. His renowned great grandfather, John Witherspoon had been the first Moderator of the Presbyterian National Assembly and later the president of Princeton University—a college where one of John's uncles was later the president. Two other uncles were, respectively, a nationally known Presbyterian minister who was Chaplain of the House of Representatives and the President of Centre College in Kentucky.

John graduated from Centre College in 1839 and shortly after that attended Princeton. Subsequently he studied at Transylvania College in Lexington, Kentucky before passing the bar examination and opening a legal practice in Lexington.

A signal event in his life occurred on July 4, 1841, when he was asked to give the major speech at the State Capitol in Frankfort. At the age of twenty he was already known as an excellent speaker but this oration was so well received that his reputation as a spell-binding orator was secured forever. (In this speech he equivocated on the slavery issue by indicating that he was personally opposed to slavery but that it was unconstitutional for the federal government to abolish it in the new territories.)

Shortly thereafter, Breckinridge returned to Lexington where he met and married Mary Burch, the daughter of a prominent family. They settled briefly in Georgetown, Kentucky before returning permanently to Lexington where he opened a law practice and the couple raised two sons. By all accounts theirs was a happy and mutually supportive relationship though Mary stayed largely out of the spotlight during John's career. Their love for one another is revealed in a remark which Mary once made: "I never saw him come without being glad, or leave without being sorry."

III

By the time of the presidential campaign of 1844, Breckinridge was widely sought as a speaker to endorse candidates. He did so on behalf of James Knox Polk. So effective were these speeches that he is sometime given credit for playing a role of some consequence in Polk's election.

In 1849, John was elected to the Kentucky House of Representatives as a Southern Democrat. He was active in that body promoting both state's rights and the power of the national government—an apparent inconsistency which would characterize most of his public service.

Two years later, in 1851, Breckinridge was elected to the U. S. House of Representatives serving two terms until 1855. In Congress he supported Stephen A. Douglas' bill to allow the new territories to decide the slavery issue for themselves. He worked hard for the passage of this law because it would nullify the so-called "Missouri Compromise" of 1820 which said that Congress could decide the question of slavery in these new lands. Thenceforth, Breckinridge was regarded—especially in the South—as a friendly pro-slavery politician.

IV

In 1856 Breckinridge, at age thirty-five, became the youngest man in history to be elected vice president of the United States. He ran on the ticket with James Buchanan although he had first supported Franklin Pierce. When Pierce fared badly in the Democratic Convention, he switched his support to Stephen A. Douglas who also failed to gain a majority at the convention. Then James Buchanan offered him the vice presidency if he would back him. Breckinridge at first declined but when he was nominated anyway, he accepted—reluctantly. In the general election, Buchanan and Breckinridge easily defeated the Republican presidential candidate, John C. Fremont.

His years in the vice presidency were probably the most unproductive and unhappy of his public life. Although he had been a critical part of Buchanan's campaign—which depended on the southern votes that

Breckinridge would deliver—Buchanan almost totally ignored his vice president. Buchanan refused to involve him in cabinet meetings or even to see him in his office, doubtless fearing that Breckinridge would be a threat to his re-election hopes if John got any of the spot-light. For the first and only time in his adult life John was virtually cut off from any influence on public affairs.

V

As the election of 1860 approached, Breckinridge decided to leave the most unproductive office he had ever held and make a try for the most important office he could imagine, the presidency. Running for this office, as a candidate of the Southern wing of the Democratic Party on an openly pro-slavery platform, he did not fare at all well in the election, finishing third to Abraham Lincoln and Stephen A. Douglas.

Immediately he ran for the U. S. Senate from Kentucky and was elected but served only from March until December, 1861. By that time, the Southern states had seceded from the Union, the Civil War had begun and he was about the only Southerner left in the Senate. His home State of Kentucky was still neutral in the War but he was branded a traitor by the Senate and fled to the Confederacy.

Jefferson Davis, the President of the new Confederate States of America, immediately made Breckinridge a general in the Confederate Army and gave him command of the first Kentucky Brigade—hoping thereby, no doubt, to bring Kentucky into the Confederacy.

Breckinridge led his troops boldly and courageously in many of the most important battles of the Civil War, including Shiloh, Bull Run and Chickamauga. In early 1865, he was named Secretary of War in the Confederate government. When General Robert E. Lee surrendered for the South in April, 1865, the U.S. government branded Breckinridge a traitor. He fled to Cuba and then to England and later Canada.

In 1868, President Andrew Johnson issued the Amnesty Proclamation. Early the next year Breckinridge returned to his home in Lexington, Kentucky. Here he practiced law and developed a keen interest in the development of railroads in the South, becoming the president of a railroad company in Kentucky.

By the early 1870's John was growing increasingly infirm with various pulmonary diseases, doubtless resulting from his earlier war wounds. He died at home in Lexington on May 17, 1875.

VI

Clearly, John Breckinridge was yet another of our vice presidents who was very important and prominent in his day but not remembered by many in our time. His memorials are few, including towns named for him in four states: Colorado, Missouri, Minnesota and Texas. There was for a short time a Fort Breckinridge in Arizona but after the Civil War its name was changed to Camp Grant. Probably the memorial that would have meant most to him is a monument dedicated to his memory at the Court House in his beloved Lexington, Kentucky.

HANNIBAL HAMLIN
(Library of Congress)

HANNIBAL HAMLIN
(1809-1891)
1861-1865
Senator Hamlin

I

DESPITE HIS MANY NOTEWORTHY accomplishments, our fifteenth Vice President is scarcely remembered at all today except, perhaps, by a few who may recall that he was one of Lincoln's vice presidents.

Hannibal Hamlin served in the U.S. Senate for twenty-five years, with many important achievements to his credit. He was also a member of the Maine legislature, the U.S. House of Representatives, Governor of Maine and Ambassador to Spain. In all of these positions he was deeply and effectively involved in the shaping of public policies during most of the nineteenth century between the presidencies of Andrew Jackson (1837) and Rutherford Hayes (1881).

II

Hannibal Hamlin was born in 1809 in the White Mountains of Maine in the small town of Paris Hill. His grandfather, Eleazer Hamlin, had named his sons "Asia," "Africa," "Europe," and "America" before settling down a bit to name his final boys (twins) Cyrus and Hannibal. His father, Cyrus, named him Hannibal in honor of his brother who was the stuff of family legend.

The story goes that when Uncle Hannibal was dying as an infant, he was saved by an Indian princess who traveled over dangerous terrain during a terrible snow storm to get healing herbs and ointments and milk to keep him alive—even though his father, Cyrus, was a medical doctor. Believable?

While still a teenager, young Hannibal had to leave preparatory school and go to work to help support his family when his father became seriously ill and lost most of his money and property. Hannibal was both a part-time land surveyor and teacher at a local school. By all reports, he was a superb teacher, even though he was unusually young and had little formal education.

By this time, Hannibal was already developing into a tall, muscular, well-dressed, young man of dark complexion—a condition that would soon cause him some grief. (While serving in the Maine legislature in 1836, he was mocked by Senator John Holmes for his dark skin and replied: "I take my complexion from nature; he gets his from the brandy bottle. I ask you, which is the more honorable"?)

Meanwhile, after opening his own law practice when his father died in 1829, Hannibal had begun to be active in state politics, campaigning as a Jacksonian Democrat for local candidates. Before long he had acquired a reputation as a superb speaker and a likely candidate for public office.

In 1833, Hamlin married Sarah Emery, the daughter of a prominent judge in Maine. The couple had four children: George, Charles, Cyrus and Sarah Jane. They enjoyed a happy marriage until Sarah died in 1855 by which time he had, with her support, enjoyed an active political career at both the state and national levels. Two years after Sarah's death, Hannibal married her half-sister, Ellen Emery, even though she was much younger than he. Again, Hamlin enjoyed a happy and supportive relationship and could rejoice in two more children: yet another Hannibal, and Frank.

III

In 1840, after serving several years in the Maine legislature, Hannibal ran for the U.S. Congress. He lost in a very close contest but won easily when he ran again in 1843. For the next thirty-three years he served in Congress, most of them in the Senate. While in Congress he strongly opposed slavery and was therefore against the so-called "gag rule" which was designed to prohibit public anti-slavery petitions to Congress. He was also against establishment of a national bank and in favor of what was called "manifest destiny"—a far-reaching plan to promote the country's growth in territory to the Pacific Ocean and from the Mexican to the Canadian borders even if this meant more war with Britain. He was the principal author of the famed "Wilmot Proviso" which barred slavery in the new territories.

In 1856, while serving in the Senate, Hamlin was elected Governor of Maine. This was a part-time post lasting for only a year and so he was free in 1857 to run again for his Senate seat. He was easily re-elected.

IV

In 1860, Hannibal ran, somewhat reluctantly, for the U.S. vice-presidency. The presidential candidate, Abraham Lincoln, did not know him at all and was not pleased with the Republican Party's selection of him as his running mate. Hamlin had been chosen by the Party for reasons of political expediency. He was from the northeastern part of the country, where his political strength lay, and he was a progressive Jacksonian Democrat—two vital factors in "balancing" the ticket and winning the election.

The question is: why did Hannibal, a life-long progressive state's-rights Democrat ever accept this offer to be the running mate of a nationalist Republican like Lincoln? We may never know the answer. Probably it was political ambition—the old "just one heartbeat away" syndrome.

In the event, as the two men got to know each other in the White House they got along well, even to the point of liking one another. Lincoln gave Hannibal a few tasks—but not much of importance, even during the Civil War when Hamlin thought he should have been given important work to aid in the preservation of the Union. This put a strain on the relationship between the two men.

When Lincoln ran for reelection in 1864, he passed over Hamlin and chose Andrew Johnson as his running mate. Historians are not sure why he did so. Perhaps he feared, with good reason, that if he chose Hamlin that would only improve his chances of succeeding him as President, a result he clearly did not want. Perhaps he saw in Johnson a more politically congenial figure who was a Southerner and yet favored war against the South if necessary to prevent the spread of slavery into the territories.

When Lincoln was assassinated on April 15, 1865, only a month after his reelection, Hamlin remained as Andrew Johnson's vice president for less than a year during which he strongly and openly opposed the new President's "Reconstruction Program" in the South.

V

Just a few years after returning to Maine, Hamlin ran, once again, for a seat in the U.S. Senate. He was elected in 1869 and served for another twelve years in his favorite position. During these years, he enjoyed good relations with President Grant but not with President Hayes, whose policies toward the defeated South he regarded as unnecessarily harsh—a continuation of Andrew Johnson's so-called "Reconstruction."

In 1881, perhaps to rid himself of Hamlin, Hayes appointed him Minister to Spain. Having spent some years helping to shape American foreign policy when he was Chair of the Senate Foreign Relations Committee, Hamlin could not resist the opportunity to see at first-hand what was going on in Europe. In Spain and the rest of Europe, he had what he regarded as one of the best experiences of his life, thoroughly enjoying the variety in the physical terrain and the chance to meet some of the world's important leaders.

VI

Returning to America after about a year abroad, Hannibal established his home in Maine. He spent the final decade of his life happily relaxing—reading, fishing, hunting, hiking. He died of a heart attack on July 4, 1891, just short of his eighty-second birthday while playing cards with friends at his favorite club in Bangor.

There are some memorials to Hannibal's life and career. These include counties named for him in North Dakota and New York, a lake in New York, statues at the U.S. Capitol in Washington and in Bangor, Maine and a library at his birthplace in Paris, Maine.

SCHUYLER COLFAX
(Library of Congress)

SCHUYLER COLFAX
(1823-1885)
1869-1873
Smiler Colfax

I

THERE CAN BE LITTLE doubt that Schuyler Colfax is one of the MOST forgotten of the vice presidents. Compared with other holders of that esteemed office, he had a modest career in government service highlighted by fourteen years in the House of Representatives, seven as Speaker of the House. Otherwise, he held no local or state offices, no significant federal office, was never an ambassador and was generally regarded in his own day as a rather insignificant public official. He was, nevertheless much liked by many for his happy, welcoming, good-natured disposition and his ever-smiling face. Indeed, if he is remembered at all it is mostly for that smile—for which, in his day, he was widely known as "Smiler Colfax."

II

Schuyler Colfax was born in New York City in 1823 but lived most of his life, from the age of thirteen, in Indiana. His grandfather, General William Wilcox was the most noteworthy member of the family, having served with George Washington during the Revolution. His father died before he was born and his mother was only seventeen. Consequently, Schuyler went to work full-time at an early age as a clerk in various stores to help support her. In 1834, she remarried and moved with her husband, George Matthews, to Indiana where Schuyler's lot improved, as his well-connected stepfather secured for him a number of minor posts in the Indiana Senate. It was at this time that the young man began to acquire a taste for public service. Also at this time he studied law though never opening a practice.

An important aspect of Colfax's life from his earliest years was the influence of religion. Once again, his stepfather was a key factor leading the boy into the Dutch Reformed Church, where he would remain a devout member for the rest of his life. He came to regard his religious faith as the grounding for all of his important decisions and to declare on many occasions that religion was the true basis of all morality. He strongly opposed the use of alcoholic beverages and was at the same time a life-long advocate of the rights of women, basing both of these "crusades" on his Christian faith. With it all, he was usually viewed not so much as a doctrinaire Christian but as a caring humanitarian.

Another of Colfax's keen interests during the earlier years of his career was journalism. In the early 1840s he began to write articles on a regular basis for local newspapers in Indiana, a practice he would continue for many years. As early as the age of sixteen he had given evidence of his talent as a journalist when Horace Greeley's *New York Tribune* began to publish his articles on a variety of subjects. When he was in the Indiana Senate he wrote regularly for the *Indiana State Journal*. In 1842 he purchased a failing newspaper, the *St. Joseph's Valley Register*. He soon made this a highly profitable paper which he edited personally for two decades.

In 1844, Colfax married Ellen Clark, a girl he had known some years earlier when he was a small boy in New York City. Apparently theirs was a happy marriage although Ellen was chronically ill and died at age of forty, several years before Colfax became vice president. The couple had no children.

III

Colfax was selected as a delegate to the National Whig Party Convention in 1848, supporting the nomination of General Winfield Scott. When Scott was defeated by General Zachary Taylor, he then campaigned energetically for him in the general election against Senator Lewis Cass of Michigan. Following Taylor's tragic death only eighteen months after taking office—he was probably poisoned by radicals supporting slavery who were disappointed by his failure to support them, Schuyler ran for Congress but lost the election. He ran again four years later and this time was elected. While in Congress, he was a powerful orator opposing the spread of slavery even when it was approved by voters living in the new Territories.

Shortly after his election to Congress, Colfax made one of the great mistakes of his career when he attended the Know Nothing Party Convention of 1855, apparently with the idea of joining the Party. By this time, this notorious Party had largely lost its influence. For anyone with serious political ambitions outside the South, it was a great mistake to have this affiliation on his resume. (In fact, the Know Nothing Party had begun in the 1840s and had ceased to be of any importance by the time of Colfax's ambitions for the White House in the late '50s. Originally an anti-Roman Catholic Party which feared what it regarded as the Roman Church's anti-democratic and authoritarian nature, the Know Nothings were soon opposing immigration as a similar threat, this time from alien cultures which they believed would injure democracy by corrupting traditional American values. When questioned about their true motives, party members would respond: "I know nothing." In 1854, they reached the apex of their power when they carried Massachusetts, nearly won New York and sent seventy-five of their members to Congress, with most of their strength in New England and the border states. In 1855 the Party changed its name to The American Party and strongly supported pro-slavery actions. Their nominee for the White House was Millard Fillmore. By the following year, as civil war approached, the Party essentially collapsed as a political influence in the country.)

One of Colfax's major contributions while serving in Congress in the late 1850s and early 60s was his work as Chairman of the Post Office Committee. Beginning in 1858, he personally supervised the complete reorganization and extension of the U.S. Postal Service.

When Lincoln was elected President in 1860, Schuyler, who had supported Stephen A. Douglas in the general election, backed the new President. As a member of Congress, he urged him to issue the <u>Emancipation Proclamation</u>. In 1865, he signed the Thirteenth Amendment to the Constitution which outlawed slavery and later said of that event that it was "the happiest day of my life."

Not long thereafter, he was invited by Lincoln to join him at a production at the Ford Theatre in Washington, something the two men often did together. Colfax, who had other plans for the evening, reluctantly declined but shook Lincoln's hand as he left for the theatre— the last public figure to do so before the assassination of the sixteenth President.

IV

In 1868, Ulysses Grant selected Colfax to be his running mate in his bid for the presidency. By this time Schuyler was well regarded as an excellent congressman with an outstanding record as Speaker of the House, which had made him a well-known public figure throughout most of the country. However, some in the Republican Party regarded him as a pleasant but superficial person who had correctly opposed slavery but was without real talent for governing. One leading Republican Senator of the day, Carl Shurz, spoke for many in his Party when he said:

Colfax is a very popular man and on this account a strong candidate. His abilities are not distinguished but are just sufficient to make him acceptable to the masses. They are fond of mediocrity.

There is little doubt that this characterization was accepted by many at the time, although probably in a somewhat more favorable light than that cast by Senator Shurz. More typically, Colfax was seen more positively as a friendly, welcoming person who might not be particularly distinguished or even capable of high achievement but could be counted on to have a warm and inviting smile on his face. Indeed, people of the day, as we have noted, often referred to him as "Smiler Colfax."

As vice president, Colfax was a reliable and capable presider over the Senate—his major responsibility—other than being prepared to take over for the president if he should die in office. Like most of his predecessors and followers in this role he found the job unfulfilling. Also, like most vice- presidents, he was largely ignored by the president whose shoes he hoped one day to fill. No doubt the happiest part of these years was his marriage to Ellen Wade whom he truly loved and who provided him with support, affection and his only child, also named Schuyler—of course.

A much less happy event of his vice presidency was the disclosure of his role in the Credit Mobilier scandal when he and other leading Republicans were accused of taking bribes from this railroad construction company. Colfax had worked for this firm during his years of active involvement with railroad construction in the west. Eventually, he admitted taking bribes in the form of shares in the company. He and the others accused were never formally charged although the scandal hurt many careers, including his own, probably dashing any last hope he may have had to be President.

V

After losing his bid for a second term as vice president in 1872, Colfax retired from public life and went home to South Bend, Indiana. He was only fifty. Though he stayed out of politics for the rest of his life, he continued to be an active public speaker, talking usually about his extensive travels and experiences in the western part of the country. In fact, it was while en route to one of these speeches in Minnesota on

January 18, 1885, after walking through a freezing rainstorm on the way to the railroad station, that he died in the station waiting room of a heart attack.

Like many other "forgotten" vice presidents, Colfax lasting memorials consist mostly of counties, towns and streets named in his honor. In his case there are ten counties located all over the country, ten towns in nine states, two schools in Pennsylvania and one statue of him in the town of Colfax, California.

HENRY WILSON
(Library of Congress)

HENRY WILSON
(1812-1875)
1873-1875
The Not So Common "Common Man"

I

THE SIMILARITIES BETWEEN HENRY Wilson and his predecessor vice president, Schuyler Colfax, are striking. Both men served under the same president, Ulysses Grant; both began their political careers as members of the Whig Party and ended them as Republicans; both had their presidential aspirations essentially wrecked because of earlier membership in the notorious Know Nothing Party; both knew Lincoln personally and worked closely with him; both strongly opposed slavery and spent their careers trying to limit or end it. And last, but not least, both were handsome men with welcoming personalities who enjoyed widespread popularity throughout much of the country.

II

Henry Wilson was born near Farmington, New Hampshire on February 16, 1812—but Henry Wilson was not his name. From birth to age twenty-one he was Jeremiah Colbath, named for his father, a no-account unskilled laborer who was drunk much of the time and failed adequately to support his wife and four sons. For most of his teen years, young Jeremiah worked as a local farmhand but by the age of twenty-one he had had enough of this life. He moved to Natick, Massachusetts and changed his name to Henry Wilson. (No one knows just why he picked this name.)

Rather quickly, Wilson found his way into the shoe manufacturing business where he remained for nearly twenty years, eventually owning his own factory and employing more than one-hundred workers. By the time he was in his early thirties, Henry was a widely known and respected businessman throughout much of New England. During these early years he found a little time now and then to attend a few local academies but not for much more than a year of formal education altogether.

III

While still active in the shoe business, Wilson entered local politics. In 1840, not yet thirty years old, he ran successfully for the Massachusetts State legislature and for the next twelve years served in either the Senate or the House of that state. It would be no exaggeration to say that he soon came to "love" the political life.

As a politician and government official, Wilson's major objective was to champion the welfare of the "common man." He always viewed himself—quite rightly—as one who had come far in life despite enormous handicaps in his family background and wished to help those with similarly unfortunate beginnings. In this regard, he pressed continuously for the development of public education and laws limiting alcohol consumption. Mostly, however, it was the institution of slavery which Wilson identified most with his own early hardships as a "common man."

The complete abolition of slavery became the principal goal of most of Wilson's political career and one may rightly say that he is one of the most important figures in the history of the long struggle to accomplish this objective in the United States. His first major achievement in this crusade was to organize a national anti-slavery political party. After a short time attempting to develop a progressive wing in the Whig party, Wilson became a principal founder of the Free Soil Party which sought to keep slavery out of the new territories acquired after the Mexican War. When this Party folded in 1854, he joined the American party, also known as the Know Nothing Party. He had nothing in common with the Know Nothings but hoped that since they controlled the Massachusetts legislature at the time they might appreciate his lending his considerable fame to their cause and reward him by electing him as the state's representative in the U.S. Senate. This is exactly what happened and thus Wilson became simultaneously a U. S. Senator and one accused thereafter of being an opportunist by supporting the Know Nothings only to further his political ambitions.

In 1855, while in the Senate, Wilson finally found a respectable national political party which shared his anti-slavery views. This was the new Republican Party within which he soon became one of the strongest of its anti-slavery advocates in Congress.

Shortly after civil war broke out at Ft. Sumter, South Carolina in April 1861, Wilson was commissioned a Colonel in the Massachusetts militia and recruited over two-thousand men for the Twenty-second Massachusetts Volunteers. Before he saw any military action, however, he resigned his commission and returned to the Senate where he served in the important post of Chairman of the Military Affairs Committee, thus playing a major role in orchestrating the government's military strategy.

As the war progressed and southerners left Congress, Wilson was able to press his abolitionist views with growing success on a somewhat reluctant President Lincoln. In 1862, he successfully guided legislation through Congress which abolished slavery in the District of Columbia. No one was happier than he when, in January, 1863, Lincoln finally issued the Emancipation Proclamation and when, in 1865, near the end of the war, Congress passed the Thirteenth Amendment abolishing slavery altogether.

Following a disappointing experience trying to work with president Andrew Johnson, who resisted his efforts to gain universal suffrage for Blacks, Wilson enjoyed a more congenial relationship with President Ulysses Grant, who was elected in 1868 and who supported the Fifteenth Amendment to the Constitution which granted the vote to all African Americans.

IV

Wilson's long-standing aspiration for the highest office in the land surfaced clearly in 1872 when he rejected the urging of some fellow Republicans to oppose Grant's re-nomination effort and support someone else. It was clear to Wilson that his most likely path to the White House was to back an embattled Grant and thereby earn his loyalty and support. In the event, the incumbent vice president, Schuyler Colfax, who had decided not to run again, suddenly changed his mind. Wilson, however, did not withdraw from the race and easily defeated Colfax thus earning the number two spot on the Republican ticket.

During the general election campaign, Wilson was attacked for his earlier association with the notorious Know Nothing Party and also for accepting stock (a "bribe") from Credit Mobilier, the government-financed construction company then building a transcontinental railroad line—which had obtained this contract by the votes of Senators like Wilson. (He had, in fact, accepted such stock but later returned it.)

Following his election as vice president, Wilson's career essentially ended. Like so many others, he found this a dismal and unrewarding position in which neither the President nor the Congress paid him much attention.

V

Wilson spent his final years as vice president occupying himself by writing a multi-volume history of the rise and fall of slavery in the United States. He was a lonely man whose wife and son had died several years earlier as had many of his close friends.

In May, 1873, Henry suffered a stroke which partially paralyzed him. About two years later he had two more such strokes in succession and died in his vice president's office in the Capitol in November, 1875.

WILLIAM A. WHEELER
(Library of Congress)

WILLIAM A. WHEELER
(1819-1887)
1877-1881
"Sterling Gold" Bill

I

SOME HAVE DISPUTED THE characterization of our sixteenth president as "Honest Abe." Few who knew him, however, would dispute the characterization of our nineteenth vice president as "Honest Bill." Although he was not noteworthy for his political accomplishments, oratorical abilities or brilliance of mind, William A. Wheeler was one of the most trustworthy, honorable and reliable political leaders in our history.

In school and college, Wheeler was a mediocre student and later an average attorney, at best. His career as a banker, railroad company executive, local and state office holder and member of Congress were similarly largely undistinguished. He rarely displayed more than an ordinary ability and a modest enthusiasm for himself or his enterprises. Nevertheless, when he died in 1887 the president with whom he had worked closely, Rutherford B. Hayes, described him as a man of "sterling gold character."

II

William Wheeler was born on January 30, 1819 in upstate New York in the town of Malone near Saranac Lake. His father, Almon Wheeler, died when he was still a teenager and his mother took in boarders to support the family. In 1838, William graduated from the prestigious Franklin Academy with a barely average academic record. He then attended the University of Vermont for just two years before dropping out. He was never anything approaching an exceptional student or even a very good one.

After college, Wheeler read for the law and became a legal apprentice for five years before opening his own practice. He was not particularly respected or sought out as an attorney. Again—just average! Nevertheless, in1846, when his long-time legal mentor, Asa Hascall, who was district attorney of the county, retired from that post, he arranged to have Wheeler appointed as his successor.

Three years later, William ran for a seat in the New York Assembly where he served two terms earning a reputation for being a reliable, well-informed and always well-prepared legislator. Soon tiring of political life, he returned home to Malone in the early 1850's and worked as head cashier in a new bank, once again earning a reputation as reliable, capable and honest—ideal characteristics for a banker. Before long Wheeler's reputation as a banker attracted the attention of the Ogdensburg and Rouse Point Railroad, a branch of the Northern New York Railroad which had a line passing through his town. Appointed a trustee and president of the Railroad, he served in these posts for eleven years.

There was one area in which Wheeler was notably active and outspoken during these years—his opposition to slavery. As civil war approached in the 1850s, he was attracted to the new anti-slavery Republican Party and helped organize a branch in upstate New York. In 1857 the Party nominated him for a seat in the State Senate and he was elected. Soon, as usual, he came to be regarded as so honest, reliable and quietly efficient that he was chosen president pro tem of that body.

In 1860, with Lincoln's election and approaching civil war, Wheeler was elected to the U.S House of Representatives, his first national office. He disliked the position and left it after one term. In 1868, however, he ran again for the first of three consecutive termsin Congress until 1876.

While in Congress, as an anti-slavery Republican, Wheeler had what was perhaps the most notable encounter of his entire career in public life. It happened in 1869 and secured for all time his reputation as an honest man of "sterling character." The event involved his brief but memorable encounter with Roscoe Conkling, the notorious boss of the corrupt political machine in New York City known as "Tammany Hall." Recognizing Wheeler's political strength in upstate New York and wishing to bring that region under the power of Tammany, thereby giving him control of the entire State, Conkling made him this offer publically:

> Wheeler, if you will act with us, there is nothing in the gift of the State of New York to which you might not reasonably aspire.

To which Wheeler publically and famously—replied:

> Mr. Conkling, there is nothing in the gift of the State of New York that will compensate the forfeiture of my self-respect.

A few years later, in 1873, another event occurred which further secured Wheeler's reputation for consummate honesty and integrity—if that was at all necessary at this point in his career. This involved the so-called "salary grab" when Congress voted itself a retroactive salary increase from $5,000 to $7,500 a year. Wheeler vigorously, but unsuccessfully, opposed the measure. When it passed, he returned his increase to the U.S. Treasury Department.

III

Wheeler made a bid for the highest political office to which he ever aspired in 1876. This was the vice presidency on the ticket with Rutherford B. Hayes.

This was to be one of the most controversial presidential elections in U.S. history. Samuel Tilden, the candidate for the Democratic Party, defeated Hayes in the general election by about 250,000 votes in the popular election and 184-165 in the Electoral College vote. But three southern States, Florida, Louisiana and South Carolina submitted two sets of ballots, one each for Tilden and Hayes. The Republican-controlled Congress then established a special Election Commission made up of eight Republicans and seven Democrats. The Commission selected Hayes in the face of Democratic Party threats that if he were elected they would filibuster in their states until a new election would be held unless he agreed. The Commission required that, if elected, he would withdraw all federal troops from the South and make major improvements in their economies and natural environments. Hayes agreed to these conditions.

During the election campaign, as he toured about the country on Hayes' behalf, Wheeler's tall, handsome and well-dressed appearance gave many the impression that he should be the one running for president. He doubtless began to have such an aspiration himself.

Once in office as vice president, Wheeler became very close to Hayes both professionally and personally—in sharp contrast to most vice president's relationships with their bosses. Hayes often sought, received and took Wheeler's advice on important matters of policy. After a term in the White House, Hayes, who had always stated his intention not to seek a second term, stepped down and the Republican Party selected James Garfield, even though many in the Party had urged the nomination of Wheeler.

IV

After attending Garfield's inauguration in March, 1881, Wheeler returned home to a gala welcoming party, including brass bands and all the trimmings of a triumphant homecoming. He and Hayes remained close friends, until Wheeler's death, through correspondence and contact with mutual friends. It was in 1885 that Hayes learned that his friend was seriously ill, suffering from increasing stomach and bowel problems, loss of physical balance and difficulty in walking. In May of 1887, Wheeler died at home. Shortly thereafter, Hayes made his public and famous remark that Wheeler was

"a rare man, sound and true. In character he was sterling gold."

In its obituary notice, the *New York Tribune*, in a similar vein, said that he was "not a man of brilliant parts but of natural sagacity and sturdy common sense with unswerving moral rectitude." Similarly, the *New York Times* wrote: "He was not an orator or great leader .... But he was above all things trustworthy."

THOMAS A. HENDRICKS
(Library of Congress)

THOMAS A. HENDRIX
(1819-1885)
March 4-November 25, 1885
Slavery Yes; Alcohol No

I

THOMAS HENDRIX HAS THE distinction of being one of only five vice presidents who served less than nine months in that august office. (The others were John Tyler, Andrew Johnson, Theodore Roosevelt and Harry Truman.)

Among Hendrix's other distinctions: he ran (unsuccessfully) for the presidency four times; he was the only vice president who had his picture put on U.S currency (the 1886 ten dollar bill); he probably had the most lavish and spectacular funeral ever accorded a vice president of the United States.

Our twenty-first vice president was one of the most effective leaders of a national political party in U. S. history. In his case it was the Democratic Party during one of the most tumultuous periods, the time before, during and immediately after the Civil War. As a Jacksonian Democrat during a period marked by intense anti-slavery rhetoric and action within the Republican Party, Hendrix was usually a vigorous opponent of the abolition of slavery and all civil rights for Black people. Throughout the country, and especially in his home state of Indiana,

Hendrix was known not so much as an effective public official as he was for being an astute politician.

II

Thomas Andrews Hendrix was born in Zionsville, Ohio on September 7, 1819. His father, John, was the owner of a successful general merchandise store and active in local politics. He was also an avid Presbyterian who helped organize the first Presbyterian Church in Indianapolis, Indiana, after he had moved his family there from Ohio early in Thomas' life. Under his father's influence, Thomas was raised a strictly observant Presbyterian who would later be one of the most vigorous advocates of prohibition of alcohol sales and consumption both at the local and national levels.

His uncle, William Hendrix, was an even larger influence on Thomas' early years than his father. As a former governor of Illinois and U.S. Representative and Senator from Indiana, he steadily steered his nephew toward a career in public life.

In 1836, Hendrix entered Hanover College—a Presbyterian school, of course! He graduated in 1841 and began to read law with several attorneys including his mother's brother, Judge Alexander Thompson. In 1843 he was admitted to the Indiana bar. Two years later he married Eliza Morgan. Their only child, Morgan, was born in 1851 but died just three years later. For her part, Eliza was a significant help to Thomas throughout his career, both as an advisor on political tactics and matters of public policy and also as a willing and cordial hostess.

III

Hendrix's career as an elected official began in 1848 when he was only nineteen years old and elected as a Jacksonian Democrat to the Indiana Assembly. Two years later he was chosen a member of the Indiana Constitutional Convention. It was here that he began to express with some fervor what would soon become his widely perceived hostility toward the Black race. He spoke out with firmness of his belief that the races should be kept as separate from one another as possible, even to the point of prohibiting Blacks from living in Indiana. The reason he gave was what he held to be the inherent inferiority of Black people. This position was popular with many Indianans at the time but nearly as many favored the elimination of slavery.

In 1851 Hendrix was elected to the U.S. House of Representatives and quickly became a supporter of Senator Stephen A. Douglas of Illinois who was probably the leading spokesman in Congress for permitting the expansion of slavery in the new western territories if the residents there wished it. At this time, Hendrix began to modify his pro-slavery potion a bit. This angered many voters in Indiana who opposed slavery altogether and there were enough of them to defeat Hendrix in his bid for reelection to the House in 1854.

For some years thereafter, Hendrix served as Commissioner of the U.S. Land Office under Presidents Pierce and Buchanan. This was an agency charged with settling disputed land claims, especially in the new western territories. Although successful in this work, especially under John Pierce who shared his views, Hendrix had an increasingly stormy relationship with Buchanan. As one who was trying to settle land claims on their merits, he ran afoul of Buchanan's desire to reward his political supporters by granting land to them—naked political patronage! By 1859 Hendrix had had enough, resigned and returned to Indianapolis to open a law practice.

Within a short time, Abraham Lincoln was in the White House and emancipation of Black slaves became the great issue of the day, with all of its possible consequences for break-up of the union and civil war. Indiana officially supported complete emancipation but Hendrix opposed it. As Chair of the State Democratic Party Convention in 1862, he not only opposed emancipation but went so far as to pronounce that Blacks should not even be allowed to serve in the military forces of the nation.

When Democrats took control of the Indiana legislature in 1863, Hendrix was elected to the U.S. Senate. In that body he was a firm "unionist" desiring to keep the southern States from seceding by allowing them to retain slavery. He strongly opposed the Thirteen Amendment, which abolished slavery, arguing that Blacks were inherently inferior to whites and slavery should therefore be allowed in states that wished it even though, he said, he personally did not like slavery as an institution.

When Lincoln was assassinated in 1865 and Andrew Johnson became President, Hendrix supported the new President's "reconstruction" programs in the south which were generally lenient and forgiving to the former slave states. He also opposed a civil rights bill designed to aid former slaves and the Fourteenth and Fifteenth Amendments to the Constitution which guaranteed suffrage and property protection to blacks. He did so on the grounds that southern states had been given no role in approving Amendments. At the same time, he continued to express his long-standing opinion that Blacks were inherently inferior and his consequent fear of black suffrage and racial intermarriage.

IV

Thomas Hendrix sought the Democratic nomination for president in 1869. His opponent was George Pendleton of Ohio who was prominent at the time for his involvement in one of the major issues of the day which concerned the gold standard and circulation of paper money. Pendleton was a leading advocate for retaining current levels of paper currency ("soft money") instead of retiring much of it from circulation in order to control inflation ("hard money" policy).

On the twenty-first ballot, Hendrix defeated Pendleton and appeared to have secured the Democratic nomination. However, at this point Pendleton withdrew and placed the name of Horatio Seymour, the Governor of New York, in nomination. On the twenty-second ballot Seymour defeated Hendrix and became the Democratic presidential nominee.

Returning to his law practice, Thomas was soon elected Governor of Indiana, supported especially by temperance advocates who liked his ongoing push for prohibition. In 1876 he tried again for the presidential nomination but New York Governor, Samuel Tilden, prevailed at the Democratic Convention with the vice presidential nomination going to a reluctant Hendrix. In the event, the Republican candidate, Rutherford B. Hayes prevailed in the general election despite the aforementioned "corrupt bargain" deal in which Hayes had made concessions to Democrats in order to avoid their threatened filibusters in several southern states.

Following this defeat, Thomas returned to private life for a few years before trying unsuccessfully for the presidential nomination another time in 1880. Four years later he made his fourth and final such attempt, this time running unsuccessfully against Grover Cleveland for the nomination. When Cleveland offered him the vice presidential spot on the ticket he accepted reluctantly. When they won the general election against the Republican ticket headed by Congressman James Blaine of Maine, Hendrix became the twenty-first vice president of the United States.

Already very ill when he became vice president, Hendrix had a poor relationship with Cleveland because this time it was he who wanted to reward his supporters with government jobs while the new president was a vigorous proponent of widespread civil service reform. The two men were rarely in contact and Hendrix was given virtually no role in the new administration.

V

After less than nine months as vice president, Hendrix died at his home in Indianapolis after several years of illness with a variety of abdominal and pulmonary maladies. One of the most elaborate public funerals ever held in Indianapolis was arranged in his honor with such notables as President Cleveland himself in attendance.

Except for an impressive gravesite monument at the Crown hill Cemetery in Indianapolis, there are no significant lasting memorials to Thomas Hendrix.

LEVI PARSONS MORTON
(Library of Congress)

LEVI MORTON
(1824-1920)
1889-1893
The "Almost" President

I

HOW AMAZING THAT ONE of the most respected and famous American leaders of the late nineteenth century should also be one of the most completely forgotten of our vice presidents. I say "amazing" not only because of the great fame of Levi Morton in his day but also because some of the events in his political career were just that—amazing!

Take, for example, his continuing effort to achieve the political office he truly coveted—the presidency of the United States. He tried and failed four times to achieve this goal. The great irony here is that on two separate occasions he could have become president with no notable effort on his part but turned down the opportunity both times. His first chance came in 1880 when James Garfield asked him to be his vice presidential running mate but he had no interest in what he regarded as a meaningless position and said, "no thanks." As we all know, if he had say "yes" to the vice presidency he would have become president when Garfield died in office less than a year later.

Similarly, in 1896, Levi rejected an offer to run for vice president on the ticket with McKinley. If he had said "yes" this time he would have been president when McKinley died shortly before his term in office had ended.

Although Morton would suffer other disappointments in his political career—such as his failing in four tries for a seat in the U.S. Senate—nothing would ever compare with the irony of his failure to achieve his true ambition. Yes—amazing.

II

Levi Parsons Morton was born on may 16, 1824 in Shoreham, Vermont. His father, Daniel, was a Congregationalist minister and his mother an uneducated housewife. The family was so strapped financially that Levi had very little formal schooling and at age fourteen left home to take a job as a clerk in a general store in nearby New Hampshire. Not long thereafter he was working in a larger general store and doing so well that the owner had him running the operation while he was still in his late teens. By the time he was in his early twenties, Levi bought the store from its owner—who was also his patron—James Beebe, a prosperous Boston merchant. In 1851, Morton and Beebe formed a joint-company which soon prospered in many growing industries including dry goods, banking, insurance and railroad construction.

In 1855, Morton moved to New York City and developed a dry goods business which prospered until the Civil War, when his many Southern clients defaulted on bills owed to him and he began to look elsewhere for career satisfaction. By this time, he had established himself as a successful and prominent leader with impressive business credentials and, most of all, as a "self-made-man" who had risen because of his own initiative and persistence—the American dream come true.

III

The first real signs of Morton's interest in a political career appeared in 1855 shortly after he married Lucy Kimball who was from a politically active family and quickly pointed him in that direction. Soon Morton was active in helping build political party organizations, first as a Whig—his wife's Party—and later with the new Republican Party.

Morton campaigned for the first Republican presidential candidate, John C. Fremont, in 1856 and remained active in the Party until his wife died in 1871 when he lost interest and withdrew into his always preferred business activities. Shortly thereafter, however, he married again, this time to another very active political lady, Anna Street, who was quickly instrumental in "pushing" him back into the political arena. Oh, those women in his life!

In 1876, Levi ran for a seat in the U.S. House of Representatives but lost in a close race. In 1878 and 1880, he was successful. While in the House he was an advocate of high protective tariffs to protect business and legislation to prohibit poor and mentally disabled people from entering the country. He also favored the gold standard over silver-backed paper money. In all of these positions, he established himself as what today we would consider a conservative Republican backer of business interests.

In 1881, Morton resigned from Congress in order to accept President Garfield's appointment of him as Minister to France. He served effectively in this post for nearly four years, improving trade relations with the French primarily by persuading them to allow American companies to place branches in their country.

1V

Somewhat reluctantly, Levi agreed to run for the number two position on Benjamin Harrison's ticket against Grover Cleveland and Allen Thurman in 1888. He won the Electoral College vote 233-168 while narrowly losing the popular vote by only about 100,000 votes out of nearly eleven million cast.

As vice president and wife, Levi and Anna were the leading social entertainers of the day in Washington, holding lavish parties attended by the most prominent political and business leaders of the city, nation and Europe.

More importantly, Levi showed himself during these years as one of the most reliable, competent and fair-minded persons ever to serve as vice president. He displayed these qualities especially well in performing his duties as presiding officer of the Senate. On a number of occasions, for example, he ruled from the chair against President Harrison's position, as well as that of almost all fellow Republicans, on a number of important issues involving voting rights and other civil liberties for Blacks in the Southern states. The so-called "Force Bill" was the major case here. This bill was intended to guarantee Blacks voting rights in the South and it was strongly favored by the President. But Morton refused to lend his support in the Senate on the grounds that this would be a very close vote and therefore would require his complete neutrality as presiding officer.

In 1892, Morton was not re-nominated for vice president on the Republican ticket. So far as we can tell, this was just fine so far as he was concerned.

V

In 1893, the Senate honored the retiring vice president with a lavish banquet held at the Arlington Hotel in Washington. On this gala occasion he was presented with a Senate resolution thanking him for:

> The dignified, impartial, courteous manner in which you have presided over the Senate.

Back home in New York, Morton ran successfully for governor of the State in 1894. True to form, he was generally thought to be trustworthy, capable, and productive in this position as well. One of the best examples of his work was a new civil service merit system for selecting state employees. Theodore Roosevelt, later governor of New York himself, said at the time that Morton was "far and away the best Governor we have had in many a day."

In 1896, Morton ran and lost again for the Republican nomination for president. His business interests, however, continued to thrive. By 1910, his company, the Morton Trust Company, had merged with another company to become the enormously successful Guarantee Trust Company.

During his final years, Morton's success and reputation seemed to soar as never before—if that were possible. He became Chairman of the Board at Guarantee Trust, President of the Metropolitan Club of New York City and was widely known as the "grand old man of Wall Street." The list goes on and on. How's that for a "forgotten man"?

Levi Morton lived to be 96! He died in May of 1920, having suffered a variety of illnesses for the last decade of his life.

ADLAI EWING STEVENSON
(Library of Congress)

ADLAI STEVENSON I
(1835-1914)
1893-1897
The Consummate Compromiser

I

ONE OF THE FEW vice presidents to regard that office as important and fully worthy of his abilities was Adlai Stevenson Sr., better known in our time as the patriarch of a prominent political family which would include his grandson, who ran twice for the presidency in the 1950's. He is otherwise one of the least remembered of all those who held the vice presidency.

Possessed of a warm and engaging personality, Stevenson was a shrewd politician who was adept at keeping everyone guessing, including the president for whom he worked, about just where he stood on the important issues of the day. He was best known and even feared in his own time for his naked use of the patronage system when, as postmaster general, he fired hundreds of postal employees all over the country and replaced them with fellow Democrats.

II

Adlai Stevenson was born in Kentucky in 1835. His father, John, was a farmer and his mother, Eliza, a stay-at-home housewife. When he was seventeen, Adlai's family moved to Illinois where he worked at his father's sawmill business in Bloomington and taught school part-time while attending Illinois Wesleyan University. Returning to Kentucky he graduated from Centre College in Danville and shortly thereafter moved back to Bloomington, Illinois and opened a law practice. It was at this time, in the early 1860's that he made his first significant entrance onto the political scene, campaigning for Stephen A. Douglas in his run for the presidency against Abraham Lincoln in 1860.

III

During the Civil War, Stevenson, by now a prominent attorney in Bloomington, helped organize an Illinois infantry regiment which saw significant action during the conflict. In 1866, he married Letitia Green, the daughter of the president of Centre College whom he had met when both had been students there years before.

For the next twenty-five years, Adlai practiced law in Illinois while also running a local coal mining and distribution company which was one of the largest employers in the region. During these years he gradually increased his involvement in local and regional politics.

In 1874, Stevenson made his first bid for political office with a successful run for a seat in the House of Representatives. He ran again in three Congressional races, winning in 1878 but losing in 1880 and 1882. During his two terms in Congress, he displayed a talent for making friends, avoiding conflict and embracing compromise solutions to difficult problems. On the key issues of the day, tariffs, currency, and expansion of railroads, he usually held closely to the Democratic Party-line of the day: opposed to anti-trust laws and high tariffs, favoring government regulation of the emerging railroad industry and taking a pro-silver rather than a gold standard position on the question of the best backing for paper currency.

In 1884, Stevenson backed Grover Cleveland in his first bid for the White House. For this support he was rewarded with the post of Assistant Postmaster General, and later, Acting Postmaster. In these posts he became perhaps the leading Democratic Party figure in the country by inaugurating one of the largest and most nakedly political patronage/power-grab schemes in our history.

What Adlai did, which was seen at the time and later as so scandalous, was to remove, without approval of the president or any other high authority in government, over 40,000 postal workers from all over the country and replace them with loyal Democratic Party members. For this bold and unprecedented act, Stevenson gained the immediate support of Democrats nationwide and became at once the number one Democratic Party operative in the country.

IV

In 1892, Grover Cleveland, not surprisingly, chose Stevenson to run with him in his bid for reelection. The two men held different views on many issues but Cleveland knew that having Adlai on the ticket would be of enormous help. The latter's charm, outstanding speaking ability, not to mention his huge following among Democrats, would virtually assure Cleveland of a second term in the White House.

Both during the campaign and later in office as vice president, Stevenson took a middle ground on contentious matters at times, even when he actually disagreed with the president. The Democratic Party of the day was badly divided on many issues and, in an effort to unify it, Adlai was pragmatic to such a degree that it was often difficult even for Cleveland to tell just where he did stand. For many, this made him appear to be opportunistic and even dishonest in his behavior as vice president.

None of this dampened Stevenson's liking for his role as vice president. Unlike many if not most of his predecessors and followers in this post, he truly respected the office. Once he said of the vice presidency that he was so fortunate to hold the position because it allowed him to preside over "the most august legislative assembly known to men."

While serving in this office, Adlai, along with his wife Letitia who was president of the Daughters of the American Revolution at the time, were one of the most important couples in Washington society. They held frequent dinner parties and lavish receptions attended by leading figures in the city and nation.

In the election of 1894 the Republican Party swept the Democrats out of both Houses of Congress in one of the largest political landslides in our history. Not surprisingly, this helped to increase tension between the two remaining Democrats of any national import in Washington—the president and the vice president who differed on a number of matters and especially on the gold versus silver issue. Cleveland now switched his earlier position to become a strong supporter of the gold standard for setting the value of paper currency.

V

Stevenson tried for the Democratic nomination for president in 1896 but lost to William Jennings Bryan who, in turn, lost the general election to William McKinley. Returning to Bloomington the following year, Stevenson remained active in local politics while resuming his law practice. In 1900 he was selected by the Democrats to run for vice president with Bryan heading the ticket again. The pair lost the election to McKinley and Theodore Roosevelt.

In 1908, Adlai ran for his last political office, narrowly losing a race for governor of Illinois. Six years later, in 1904, he died at his home in Bloomington at the age of seventy-nine.

GARRET AUGUSTUS HOBART
(Library of Congress)

GARRET HOBART
(1844-1899)
1897-1899
The First "Modern" Vice President

I

ALTHOUGH GARRET HOBART WOULD rank among the very least remembered of the long list of "forgotten" vice presidents, he is usually regarded as the first one to set the tone and style for most subsequent holders of that office. In this sense he may be called the first "modern" vice president.

Always a businessman and private citizen first, Hobart viewed politics and government service as something of an afterthought in his life and career. Very much a son of New Jersey, he was a constant booster for his home state in almost everything he did. A staunch Republican, he consistently advocated the gold standard as what he saw as the only basis for a dependable currency and a strong nation. He also supported high tariffs to protect national business from foreign imports and a strong central government *viz- a- viz* state's rights in the development of a national railroad system and other major economic challenges.

Throughout his career, Hobart was regarded as a man of good conscience, reliable integrity and great industry. Neither imaginative or change-oriented, he was a solid supporter of the status quo in the rather stable era of the late nineteenth century.

II

Garret Hobart was born in Long Branch, New Jersey on June 3, 1844, the second of three sons of Addison and Sophia Vandermeer Hobart. Addison was a farmer and teacher who had descended from the earliest settlers in New England. He had founded an elementary school in Long Branch which was attended by all of his children. He was also involved in New Jersey politics as an active member of the Democratic Party. Sophia was from a family of early Dutch settlers in New Amsterdam (New York City).

After attending several schools in New Jersey, where he was always an outstanding student, Garret entered Rutgers College, graduating in 1863. Subsequently, he studied law and was admitted to the New Jersey bar in 1871. While in school during the 1860s, he never volunteered for military service during the Civil War but did become increasingly active in the New Jersey Democratic Party.

In 1869, Hobart married Jennie Tuttle, the daughter of Socrates Tuttle, one of his law tutors and a leading Republican politician and office holder in Passaic County, New Jersey, and a long-time mayor of Patterson. The marriage led to Garrets almost immediate conversion from the Democratic to the Republican Party.

III

Notably successful in his New Jersey business career, Hobart was president of the Passaic Water Company and Director of the First National Bank of Newark. He also held high posts in the New Jersey Midland Railroad and several smaller area businesses. He was a very wealthy man.

Occasionally during his business career, Garret would become involved in local and regional politics—not as a major interest but as what he saw as his responsibility as a community leader. During the 1880s, for example, he served as Chair of the New Jersey Republican Committee and was a delegate from the State to several national Republican Party Conventions. In 1883, he made his first of only two bids for public office when he ran for the U. S. Senate. He lost.

Following the national economic collapse in 1883, the Republican Party took control of all levels of New Jersey government. Hobart began to speak out with increasing frequency on such topics as the importance of a strong national government, high tariffs and the gold standard —the major Republican bi-words of the day. Before long, he was being seriously mentioned as a possible candidate for the vice presidency. He was willing to consider the prospect but made it clear that, even if elected, he would never give up his business interests but take them with him to Washington. And that is just what he did.

IV

President McKinley and the Republican national leadership liked the idea of Hobart as a running mate for McKinley in 1896 for several reasons. Firstly, New Jersey was a key State in prospects for victory and no one was better positioned than Hobart to deliver that state for the Republican ticket. Secondly, Hobart had absolutely no ambition to become president and hence was no threat to McKinley's aspiration for a second term. In addition, Hobart was a non-controversial figure of great wealth who was willing to supply badly needed financial support for the national ticket.

Once nominated, Hobart campaigned actively, especially in New Jersey and New York. Although he did not do so by traveling about the area—much less the country—and meeting voters personally, he did effectively use the principal method of his day, the "front-porch" campaign. In this manner he talked from home with a nation-wide radio audience about McKinley's strengths, and his own.

The major political issue of the day was the gold versus the silver standard for backing paper currency. Southern and western states generally favored the raw material that abounded in their sections of the country—silver. Easterners preferred the gold standard. Hobart said that a great nation needed a solid and fixed basis for its currency and silver was certainly not that with its constantly fluctuating market value. Only gold would do.

When the Democratic Party's presidential candidate, William Jennings Bryan, made his still famous proclamation that we "must not crucify the nation on a cross of gold," Hobart replied:

> An honest dollar, worth 100 cents everywhere, cannot be coined out of 53 cents of silver plus a legislative fiat. Such a debasement of our currency would inevitably produce incalculable loss, appalling disaster and national dishonor.

This sentiment, though less enduring than Bryan's stirring rhetoric, carried the day. McKinley was only a lukewarm supporter of the gold standard and wanted some sort of compromise solution to the currency issue—as he did on most difficult matters—but Hobart stood firm and prevailed in the administration.

In the election of 1896, the Republicans, as we have seen, won everywhere, taking not only the presidency and both houses of Congress but most major offices in the country outside the South and parts of the West. Within four years, the Gold Standard Act was passed and the great currency issue of the day resolved in large measure due to the persistence of Vice President Hobart.

As he readied himself to take over the vice presidency, during the months after the election, Hobart studied carefully the history of the office and how it had been conducted by all who had held it in the past. He also memorized the names of all the current senators so that he might preside over the Senate in a personal manner. He was, by all accounts, outstanding in his performance as presiding officer.

There can be no doubt that Hobart, unlike most of his predecessors, truly enjoyed being vice president. He spent most of his days in the Senate chambers, even when that body was not in session. He often attended committee meetings and enjoyed lunch with senators in their dining room as he struck up personal relations and even friendships with many of them.

Throughout his vice presidential term, Garret was a close friend of President McKinley who consulted him regularly in his office in the White House on matters of public policy to such an extent that Garret was referred to by many at the time as the "Assistant President." Often his wife, Jennie, filled in as hostess for the First Lady and the foursome spent many happy times together in Washington and in their later lives as well.

Most notable in Hobart's support of McKinley was his involvement in critical foreign policy actions involving the resolution of the Spanish American War over independence for Cuba. When the U.S. battleship *Maine* exploded in Havana Harbor in 1898, the question of the day was: "Did Spain do it?" And, if so, did this mean that we should declare war on Spain?

One of the men blamed as primarily responsible for the poor relations with Spain at this time, and therefore as largely responsible for bringing on the war itself, was a very close personal friend of Hobart—Secretary of War, Russell Alger. Because McKinley, as usual, wished to avoid any embarrassment for himself, he dispatched Hobart to confront his friend, Alger, and tell him that he was fired from his cabinet position. With great emotional pain, Hobart, as always loyal to the President, did as he was bid. The anguish, both mental and physical, which this caused him was deep and long-lasting and may have hastened his death.

V

Just a year later, in 1899, he suffered a severe heart attack from which he never recovered. He died at his home in Long Branch, New Jersey shortly thereafter. He was fifty-five years old.

There are very few memorials to Garret Hobart apart from a large statue of him in Patterson, New Jersey. Perhaps this is not surprising given that the era in American history to which he belonged was itself largely overshadowed by the greater events of the Civil War and its immediate aftermath and the long period of American growth and power from one Roosevelt to another which followed it.

Hobart's lasting memorial is the pattern he set for the behavior of future vice presidents: remain largely out of the public eye; have no apparent aspiration for the presidency; provide intelligent, non-public advice to the president when asked for it; be especially prepared to serve quietly in difficult overseas foreign policy assignments; generally to serve as a very low-key "assistant to the president."

Think: Joseph Biden, Richard Cheney, Al Gore, Daniel Quayle, Walter Mondale, etc., etc., etc.

CHARLES WARREN FAIRBANKS
(Library of Congress)

CHARLES FAIRBANKS
(1852-1918)
1904-1909
The "Indiana Icicle" or "Cocktail Charlie"

I

THESE TWO WIDELY USED phrases to describe Charles Fairbanks during his long business and political career—*"Indiana Icicle* and *Cocktail Charlie*—reveal his seemingly split personality. At times he was the "life of the party" and at other times cold and unresponsive: one minute a social icicle and the next, a lover of cocktail parties.

One side of our twenty- second vice president's personality was the reserved, non-expressive, behind the scenes and often secretive lawyer/ businessman who made a small fortune in railroad companies in Ohio and Indiana. His other side was the often ebullient public speaker and campaigner who seemed to enjoy all of the hoopla of politics. The first aspect of his persona served him well as a conservative Republican, who firmly and effectively but not noisily opposed all social welfare policies of the national government, especially Teddy Roosevelt's "Square Deal" programs. His other side was revealed in his efforts to gain high national office, displaying a highly effective political personality, likeable, good at hosting lively parties, "shaking hands" and making friends.

Which one was the real Charles Fairbanks? Maybe we will discover the true man by having a closer look at his personal life and public career, or maybe not!

II

Our twenty-sixth vice president was born on May 11, 1852 in a log cabin near Delaware, Ohio. His ancestors were English Puritans who had come to the Colonies in 1632. When he was a small boy during the Civil War, his father, an abolitionist, used their house to hide run-a-way slaves.

After attending several local schools as a boy, Charles entered Ohio Wesleyan University and graduated with honors in 1822. Two years later he earned his law degree from the Cleveland Law School. In that same year he married Cornelia Cole, a fellow student at Ohio Wesleyan and the daughter of a local judge. Cornelia's uncle, Charles Smith, found Fairbanks a position as an attorney in the firm where he worked, the Chesapeake and Ohio Railroad System. Thereafter, Charles held similar posts in several other railroad companies in Ohio and Indiana and became a well regarded and wealthy business figure by the time he was in his sixties and began to show a serious interest in state and national politics.

Indiana, at this time, was considered by both national political parties as essential for their success in presidential elections. This meant that each party would often select a leading figure from that State to run for the vice presidency. Indiana became known as "Mother of Vice Presidents."

In 1888, Fairbanks campaigned vigorously for Benjamin Harrison but only after he had helped his favorite, Judge Walter Gresham, carry Indiana in the primary. In 1892, Harrison lost his re-election bid to Grover Cleveland. At about this time, Fairbanks, who was now in complete control of the Indiana Republican Party organization, became acquainted with the man who largely controlled the Party in neighboring Ohio. His name was William McKinley and the two were soon close friends.

When McKinley ran for the White House four years later, Fairbanks was instrumental in delivering Indiana in a successful election campaign. With the new president's urging and assistance, Fairbanks then sought and won a seat in the U.S. Senate.

While his career in the Senate was rather lackluster with little of note accomplished, he did remain close to President McKinley by serving as his personal advisor on such critical matters as conducting a successful military campaign against Spain in the Spanish-American War. In 1898, while still in the Senate, he went to Alaska, at McKinley's request, as a member of a special commission to negotiate a settlement with England in a dispute over the Alaskan boundary. Although no formal agreement was reached at the time, Fairbanks managed to so impress Alaskan leaders—as well as much of the general public—that he became a favorite son of the region and would later have the capitol city of the new State named in his honor.

III

Having failed in a vigorous effort to achieve the Republican presidential nomination in 1904, Fairbanks reluctantly supported Teddy Roosevelt in the general election. In part for this effort and, more importantly perhaps, to balance the ticket with a conservative mid westerner, the Republican Convention selected him as Roosevelt's running mate. Although Fairbanks worked hard on the campaign trail, he was never to become close to the new president.

During his four years as vice president, Fairbanks actually opposed some of Roosevelt's most important initiatives. More faithful to his own conservative positions than his role as the president's loyal assistant, he worked assiduously to defeat Roosevelt's "Square Deal" program with its emphasis on extensive social welfare benefits.

The two men also clashed often at public events, making sarcastic remarks about one another. For example, in 1907 Roosevelt attended a party at Fairbank's home in Indianapolis where some forty guests were divided into two groups —one hosted by Fairbanks and one by Roosevelt. The menu for the affair included "Manhattan" cocktails. Remarkably, this simple reference to alcohol at a reception for the president created a national scandal—fed, of course by the news media—which led to a new popular name for Fairbanks. Henceforth he was known as "Cocktail Charlie."

It is doubtful that Fairbanks ever actually had a drink, as he was a confirmed teetotaler. Nevertheless, Roosevelt delighted in branding his political enemy an alcoholic. Toward the end of his term, at a party in his honor at the Gridiron Club in Washington, he was very sarcastic in remarks blaming Fairbanks for the entire "affair."

IV

In 1908, when Roosevelt was preparing to leave the White House, Fairbanks entertained serious hopes of replacing him. But Roosevelt vigorously opposed his nomination and supported William Howard Taft as his successor.

Shortly after leaving Washington Fairbanks and his wife, Cornelia took a trip around much of the world. On a stop in Rome they hoped to visit the Pope but that august personage refused them an audience. It seems they had had the temerity to stop first at several Methodist schools in the city. Returning to his law practice in Indiana, Fairbanks served as a trustee at his alma mater, Ohio Wesleyan University, and several other colleges as well. By an act of Congress in 1882 he was named a regent of the Smithsonian Institution.

In 1916 Fairbanks ran for the vice presidency again, this time on the Charles Evans Hughes presidential ticket. The pair lost to Woodrow Wilson and Thomas Marshall. Two years later, Fairbanks died at his home of nephritis.

There are few lasting memorials to Charles Fairbanks, the most notable being the city of Fairbanks, Alaska, along with a few other cities named in his honor in Minnesota, Oregon and Michigan.

JAMES SCHOOLCRAFT SHERMAN
(Library of Congress)

James S. Sherman
(1855-1912)
1909-1912
"Sunny Jim"

I

THERE ARE NO LASTING memorials to our twenty-seventh vice president, not even a short biography. James Schoolcraft Sherman is among the most "forgotten" men who have ever held the #2 post in our government. As a political leader in Congress for twenty years and vice president for one term, he originated very little of importance. His interests ran more to the "how" than to the "what" or "why" of public policy. At heart, he was a parliamentarian not a legislator.

On the plus side, Sherman was good-natured, non-combative and approachable in an era of controversy and conflict within the Republican Party. These were the years when the feisty, rambunctious Teddy Roosevelt and his controversial "Square Deal" social welfare agenda dominated the political scene, to be followed by the only slightly less controversial presidency of William Howard Taft. In the midst of this, Sherman was a leading conservative who represented what many then and now view as the true nature of the Republican Party.

II

James Sherman was born in 1855 in Hartford Village, New York, a small suburb of Utica. His father, Richard Updike Sherman, was an active Democrat who served for many years as the chief clerk in the U. S. House of Representatives and authored the legislative manual for the House which was in use until very recently. The Shermans were descendants of Roger Sherman, a signer of the Declaration of Independence and William Tecumseh Sherman, a leading Union general during the Civil War.

In 1878 James graduated with a bachelor's degree from Hamilton College and a year later received his law degree from that same highly respected institution. Shortly after opening his law practice in Utica, he married Carrie Babcock whom he had known since childhood. Pretty and talented, she was supportive of his business career and political ambitions and was also politically active in her own right. For example, while he was in Congress, she formed the Congressional Club for Wives of Congressman.

III

During the decades of his career before he ran for public office, Sherman was a well-known business leader in both Connecticut and New York. When his father died in 1895, he assumed the presidency of the New Hartford Canning Company. Soon, he was instrumental in creating the Utica Trust and Deposit Company which became one of the most important financial institutions in the northeast.

Shortly after his marriage, Sherman was drawn into politics. In 1884, he was, not surprisingly, elected mayor of Utica. He accomplished nothing of note during his short time in this office. Just three years later he was elected to Congress and remained there until his death, twenty years later, in 1912.

Sherman was never a leader in Congress during his many years as a member. He initiated virtually no legislation of consequence. Like his father, who as previously noted had written the manual on how to enact laws, Charles was a parliamentarian—not a legislator. He was, nevertheless, highly regarded by his Congressional colleagues, not only for his skill as a parliamentarian but also for his unfailing good nature, almost totally non-argumentative. He was soon given the moniker: "Sunny Jim."

Sherman was also regarded by commentators of the day as one of the "big five" in the House, along with Speaker, Joe Canon of Illinois, Sereno Payne of New York, John Dulzell of Pennsylvania and James Tawney of Minnesota. Some later historians, however, have described his congressional career in much less flattering terms. Taft's biographer, Henry Pringle, called him "a conservative political hack" and author, William Manners, said that "during his twenty years in the House [he] had done not a single thing of value."

IV

Apparently against his will—certainly without any noticeable enthusiasm—Sherman accepted his Party's nomination as William Howard Taft's running mate in 1908. The pair easily defeated Democrat William Jennings Bryan.

As vice president, Sherman displayed the same low-key, non-productive, good natured persona which he had shown throughout his political career. One major exception to this posture was his vigorous activity in the area of policy toward Native Americans. As Chair of the House Committee on Indian Affairs, he sought to break up the tribes and treat all Native Americans as a single group. Not surprisingly, this effort did not go over well with most Native Americans. They were probably delighted when Sherman was accused, probably justly, of the only major wrong-doing of his public career. At the time it was alleged and widely believed but never proved that he had engaged in the secret sale of oil from Indian lands in order to secure money to pay for his political campaigns.

Philip Secor

Halfway through Sherman's first term as vice president, his Republican Party was fractured when Teddy Roosevelt broke away and formed his own Bull Moose Party. Taft and Sherman were then nominated again by what remained of the Republican Party but lost to Woodrow Wilson in a not-surprising Democratic landslide.

V

Since about 1908, Sherman had been suffering badly from Bright's Disease, a serious kidney ailment. He gave his vice presidential acceptance speech in 1912 while very weak from the ailment. On October 30th, just days before the general election, he died, leaving Taft without a vice presidential running mate.

In his funeral oration, Taft summed up Sherman's public career as follows:

Those who know him loved him; those who knew the services he rendered to his county respected him."

Of course not many now or then, knew him at all.

Thomas Riley Marshall
(Library of Congress)

THOMAS RILEY MARSHALL
(1824-1925)
1913-1921
"The Most Popular Vice President"

I

PERHAPS, AS WE SHALL see, our twenty-eighth vice president was the most popular to hold that office. But he was also one of the most "forgotten." Probably best remembered, if at all, for his wry comment: "What this country really needs is a good five-cent cigar," Thomas Marshall was indeed a prolific smoker, rarely seen without a huge stogie either protruding from his mouth or extended and gestured from his hand to emphasize some point or other.

Some historians have, however, somewhat questionably I think, credited Marshall with the enormous achievement of having been the true author of the Twenty-fifth Amendment to the Constitution which was not enacted until 1967, nearly half a century after his death. The argument is that because, while vice president, he was cautious and refused to assume the presidency during Woodrow Wilson's long illness, thereby causing confusion about who really was running the country, it needed to be made lawful for future vice presidents to simply assume the presidency under such circumstances which is what the Twenty-fifth Amendment does.

II

Thomas Riley Marshall was born on March 14, 1854 in North Manchester, Indiana, not far from Fort Wayne. His maternal grandfather, Riley Marshall, became wealthy when, after oil and natural gas were discovered on his farm, he sold the property for nearly half-a-million dollars (today's dollar value). He subsequently became a leader in the state Democratic Party, serving as party chairman and state senator. His considerable means allowed him to send his only son, Daniel—Thomas' father—to medical school. In 1848, Daniel married Martha Patterson, a lovely woman whose wit and charm were no doubt "inherited" by her son. Unfortunately, Martha contracted tuberculosis and suffered badly from the disease while Thomas was a boy.

Thomas attended public elementary school in Fort Wayne before entering Wabash College in Crawfordsville in 1870—an Indiana education throughout! Not only Indiana, but Presbyterian. The Marshalls were devout and active members of that church and earnestly wished Thomas to become an ordained Presbyterian minister. It was not to be. At Wabash College, the young man, who made a superb academic record, was active in campus social life, graduated with a Phi Beta Kappa key and became interested in law and politics. As a writer for the student newspaper, *The Geyser*, he wrote an article criticizing a visiting lecturer. When that person sued him for defamation of character, Thomas managed to convince none other than future president William Henry Harrison, at that time a prominent attorney in Indianapolis, to defend him—successfully as it turned out.

After reading law for some time, Marshall was admitted to the bar—in Indiana of course—and began what would soon be one of the most successful practices in the state. As his fame and popularity spread, he began to show an interest in politics.

In 1895, at the age of forty, Marshall married Lois Kinsey, who had been a clerk in her father's law office and was nearly twenty years his junior. Theirs was a happy and mutually supportive relationship, though frequently marred by Thomas' severe alcohol addiction. (When Kate Hooper, the woman he had hoped to marry many years earlier died just before their marriage, he took to heavy drinking which became a major problem for the rest of his life.) Without the steady help and support of Lois, he probably would have had no public career at all.

III

Marshall's political career began in earnest in 1908 with his successful run for governor of Indiana. Not surprisingly, he won easily. His state-wide popularity, good looks and charm made his victory—as well as his re-election to a second term in 1910—virtually a foregone conclusion.

His record as governor was outstanding and he remained throughout an independent Democrat who refused to follow dictates from the party's powerful political machine as he charted his own course in public policy development. His was a progressive reform program including child labor laws, public health, railroad safety and, most controversially, prison reform. So aggressive was he in efforts to improve conditions in prisons and in the life of inmates generally, with special emphasis on elimination of the death penalty and improved prospects for pardon, that he was soon known as the "pardoning governor."

The story goes that one day, while walking in a crowd, he was pushed rather hard by a man who said to him: "Pardon me" and Marshall purportedly replied: "Certainly; but what crime have you committed?"

Thomas' major goal as governor was to rewrite the State constitution in such a way as to further his progressive agenda, with special emphasis on encouraging and protecting labor unions and, in any way possible, promoting so-called "direct democracy, i.e., the use of voter initiative and referendum as part of law-making. His proposed constitution was, to say the least, controversial. Some compared it disparagingly to the ideas of Socialist leader, Eugene Debs. Challenged in both state and federal courts, including the U.S. Supreme Court, Marshall's plan was never approved.

IV

In 1912 Marshall was nominated by the Democratic Party to run for the vice-presidency on the ticket with Woodrow Wilson. The campaign against former president, Theodore Roosevelt, was fierce and nasty with Marshall making most of the vigorously negative attacks. In the event, Wilson and Marshall won overwhelmingly.

Wilson never liked his vice president, gave him little of consequence to do, avoided him as much as possible and even went so far as to do the unthinkable—subverting Marshall's only constitutional prerogative which was to preside over the Senate and be, if he liked, something of a leader of that body. Wilson did this by holding his own private meetings with senators, both in his office and theirs, thus stripping Marshall of all but the limited parliamentary function of presiding at Senate meetings.

Marshall was, however, most effective in performing this function. This was a time of important and controversial legislative initiatives designed to overhaul the entire financial system of the country. The Federal Reserve and Underwood Tariff Acts of 1913 and The Clayton Anti-trust Act of 1914 are examples of the laws which Marshall successfully—with even temper and fairness to both sides of usually contentious argument—shepherded through the Senate.

Not unlike most of his predecessors and successors, Vice President Marshall viewed his office as essentially inconsequential—except, of course, for the hope of one day stepping into the presidency. He liked to tell the tale of two sons, one of whom went to sea and drowned while the other entered politics and became vice president. He never heard from either of them again.

In 1916, Marshall was re-elected with Wilson but never really supported the president's move toward U.S. involvement in World War I. The important aspect of his second term as vice president was that he was called upon to act as president without ever officially serving a single day in that office.

While Wilson was travelling abroad after the war and, more importantly, when he became seriously ill with a prolonged illness after returning home in 1919, Marshall was called upon to perform most of his official duties. The problem was that Wilson's wife, Edith, as well as Wilson's friends and advisors, disliked and distrusted the vice president. They, with the connivance of the president's doctors, hid his illness from the general public and attempted to run the government secretly as though Wilson were still in charge. Later this became known as Edith Wilson's "petticoat government."

Many of Marshall's friends urged him simply to assume the presidency. He declined, arguing that there was no constitutional warrant for him to do so. (Not until 1962 would the 25th Amendment grant the vice president the constitutional right to assume the presidency under such circumstances.) Instead, Marshall did his best for nearly two years (September 1919 to March 1921), to remain loyal to Wilson's goals, whether or not he personally approved—including support for a new international organization called The League of Nations.

V

When he left Washington and returned to Indiana in 1922, Marshall opened a law practice in Indianapolis and began to write his memoirs, including such books as *Recollections of Thomas Marshall, Vice President* and *Hoosier Philosopher: A Hoosier Salad.* (This work became an important part of the country's historical record for the late nineteenth and early twentieth centuries) During these years he also served as a trustee of his alma mater, Wabash College.

On June 1, 1925, Marshall died of a heart attack while in bed reading the Bible. His important legacy is the 25th Constitutional Amendment regarding presidential succession. According to some historians, this vital provision might never have been enacted—even if belatedly—had it not been for Marshall's indecisiveness during Wilson's long illness. On the other hand, some commentators have been sharply critical of Marshall for not simply assuming the presidency during such difficult times in the country without being so influenced by strict

Constitutional correctness. One historian, Samuel Eliot Morison, has gone so far, in fact, as to blame Marshall, indirectly, for the rise of Hitler and onset of World War II which, he argues, might never have occurred had Marshall assumed the presidency and secured ratification of the League of nations.

Another writer, Claire Suddath, in the August 21, 2008 issue of *Time Magazine,* has gone so far as to call Marshall one of the worst vice presidents in U.S. history. On the other hand, another commentator, John V. Hicks, has described him as "perhaps the most popular president we have ever had."

Is it possible to do a poor job in high public office and still be popular with the general public? You bet it is!

CHARLES GATES DAWES
(Library of Congress)

CHARLES GATES DAWES
(1865-1951)
1925-1929
"Hell and Maria" Dawes"

I

NOBEL PEACE PRIZE WINNER, war hero, congressman, nationally respected business leader and vice president of the United States, Charles Gates Dawes is one of the most forgotten of our leaders from the past.

He is best remembered, if at all, for an angry remark he made when testifying before Congress in 1921 for alleged careless spending in the procurement of military supplies during World War I—a task assigned him by President Woodrow Wilson. He screamed at the Committee:

"Hell and Maria, we weren't trying to keep a set of books; we were trying to win a war."

Henceforth, he was known as "Hell and Maria Dawes."

II

Charles Gates Dawes was born in Marietta, Ohio in August, 1865. His father, Rufus, was a Republican congressman for one term: 1881-1883. Charles graduated with a degree in civil engineering from Marietta College in 1884. While in college, he developed a strong interest in music and would one day become a pianist of some note.

After receiving an LLB degree from Cincinnati Law School in 1886, Dawes practiced some law but was soon engaged in a career as a civil engineer, for a short time working for a leading railroad company in Ohio. In 1887 he moved to Lincoln Nebraska to work for the law firm of his cousin, James Dawes, who had been governor of that State. There he met and soon became close friends with William Jennings Bryan, who had his office in the same building.

In 1889, Charles married Caro Blymer, whom he had known while in law school in Cincinnati. The couple had four children—two of them adopted—and enjoyed an apparently congenial and mutually supportive relationship. Caro died in 1953, two years after the death of her husband.

The couple moved to Chicago in 1895 where Charles began a long and notable career as a consultant to many companies by helping them to improve their operations, often by means of extensive reorganization. This work was so successful that he soon became well-known and respected and was drawn into Illinois politics. He campaigned for William McKinley in the 1896 presidential election as a leader of the reform wing of the Republican Party in Illinois and successfully delivered the State's electoral votes to him. He was rewarded with the position of Comptroller of the U.S. Currency, a post he held until 1901.

In that year, Dawes ran unsuccessfully for the U. S. Senate. He would have been elected had McKinley not been assassinated and replaced in the White House by Theodore Roosevelt who generally disapproved of the Republican Party leadership in Illinois.

During World War I Dawes volunteered for the army and was a member of the American Expeditionary Force fighting in France. In 1918 he was promoted to the rank of brigadier general and put in charge of all military purchases overseas. (After the war he wrote a book on this activity.)

In 1921, Congress conducted an investigation of military spending during the war. Many of the Republican members saw the war itself as unnecessary and blamed the Democrats in general and Dawes in particular for its inception. During the lengthy and acrimonious hearings, Dawes often lost his temper, screaming and waving his arms and hands at the Investigating Committee. At one point, in the midst of one of his tirades, he shouted:

Sure we paid. We didn't dicker. Damn it all, the business of the army is to win the war not to quibble around with a lot of cheap buying. Hell and Maria, we weren't trying to keep a set of books; we were trying to win the war.

And so Dawes became known as "Hell and Maria Dawes." (The term itself was one he frequently used when angry and probably referred to the Virgin Mary.) The remark was repeated so often by a delighted press that Dawes was soon far more famous throughout the country than he had ever been before—so much so that he was seriously considered for the presidency on the Republican ticket in 1920. He wasn't selected but shortly thereafter the new president, Warren G. Harding, appointed him Director of the Budget.

So outstanding was his work reorganizing the Budget Bureau to make it more effective that the agency has remained in much the same excellent condition to the present day.

In 1924, Charles became engaged in what is probably the most notable work of his career in public service. He developed and applied what came to be known as the "Dawes Plan" for rebuilding and stabilizing the government and economy of post-war Germany. His conciliatory and effective approach to working with America's and Europe's former enemy earned him the Nobel Peace Prize.

III

Dawes was selected by the Republican Convention in 1924 to be Calvin Coolidge's running mate in his bid for a second term in the White House. Coolidge himself had no hand in the selection and never really liked Dawes, even though Charles campaigned vigorously for him in the landslide victory over Democratic candidates, John Davis and Charles Bryan.

Coolidge's cool behavior toward Dawes intensified to outright dislike when, as he saw it, Dawes upstaged his Inaugural Address in which he had planned to set forth an agenda for the country in a highly dramatic Inaugural speech. Dawes' address was a fierce and newsworthy tirade against the Senate. In this, his latest intemperate outburst, Dawes screamed at the Senate, demanding a total reform of its procedures. The members were, of course, deeply offended and at least as angry with him as was the president. The press, of course, was delighted and its coverage of Dawes did, indeed, overshadow any attention to the President's address.

The breach between Dawes and Coolidge was complete when Dawes failed to appear in the Senate to break what seemed at the time to be a certain tie vote on whether to approve Coolidge's nomination for Attorney General of Charles Warren. Dawes, is seems, had left the Senate chamber, assured that the fierce debate over the nomination would not end for many hours, and returned to his headquarters at the Willard Hotel to relax. But the final vote came more quickly than expected and Warren was defeated by one vote. Coolidge never forgave Dawes. Thereafter, Dawes did little in the Senate other than to oppose many of Coolidge's legislative initiatives.

At the 1928 Republican Convention, Dawes was nominated for the presidency but received only four votes. The nominee, Herbert Hoover, did not support him in his bid for the vice presidential nomination and so he lost that spot as well.

For a number of years thereafter Charles turned his attention to foreign affairs. In 1928, he was invited by President Horatio Vasques of the Dominican Republic to head a commission to revise the finances of that new country. He did so in short order and with good long-term results. In 1929, he accepted Hoover's appointment as ambassador to Great Britain. In this post he played an important part in discussions leading to the Conference on Naval Limitation in 1930.

Dawes final public positions were in 1932: first as one of those helping to organize and finance the Chicago World's Fair, known as the Century of Progress, and then, briefly, as Hoover's first president of the Reconstruction Finance Corporation (RFC) which was a precursor of FDR's New Deal by providing federal government loans to businesses nearing financial collapse.

IV

By 1933, with the economic depression in full bloom, Dawes completely withdrew from public life. He was back in Chicago tending his business interests, including what would be the most controversial and damaging act of his life: the securing of a $90 million personal loan from the RFC just after he had resigned the presidency of that organization. This deed seriously damaged his reputation.

Dawes spent the last two decades of his life recounting his long career in public life in a number of diary-like books including *Notes as Vice President* (1935), *A Journal as Ambassador to Great Britain* (1939) and *A Journal of the McKinley Years* (1951). During these final decades he also served as Chairman of the Board of the City National Bank and Trust Company of Chicago.

V

Charles Gates Dawes died at home in Evanston, Illinois on April 23, 1951. He was eighty-five. Some historians, noting especially his Nobel Peace Prize for helping settle European affairs after the War and his outstanding service as a financial manager after the Great Depression, have rated him among our best vice presidents. Robert Waller, a retired professor and dean at Clemson University has, for example, recently described him as a "near great" vice president who "stands among the luminaries" who have occupied that office. (Edward Purcell, ed., *Vice Presidents*, Checkmark Books, 2001, 281.)

CHARLES CURTIS
(Library of Congress)

CHARLES CURTIS
(1860-1936)
1929-1933
Our Only Native American Vice President

I

CHARLES CURTIS IS THE only person of Native American ancestry ever to serve as vice president. His mother, Ellen Pappan, was of one-quarter percent Indian blood and a member of the Kaw Tribe in Kansas. Charles was raised in the tribal village by his maternal grandparents until the age of fourteen when the tribe moved to Oklahoma and he opted to remain in Kansas with his Caucasian relatives.

Curtis was a long-time U.S. congressman from his home town of Topeka, Kansas, serving in the House from 1893-1907 and in the Senate from 1914-1929. In the Senate he was an influential figure, serving for his final four years as Majority Leader. He found his role as a congressman fully engaging and was for all of these years a popular and well-regarded public official. Like most of his predecessors and followers, he was bored by the vice presidency except, in his case, grateful for the opportunity it provided for continued political activity, social entertaining and public notice—and also, of course, in the hope that it might lead him directly to the presidency.

II

Charles Curtis was born in January 1860 in Topeka, Kansas Territory, the year before Kansas was admitted to the Union as a State. His mother, as noted, gave him his Native American lineage and his early life in an Indian tribe. She died when he was three and his father, Orren Curtis, then married two other women in rapid succession. Orren was later imprisoned during his service as a Union officer in the Civil War for a serious infraction of military law.

For most of his childhood, Charles was raised by his maternal grandparents on the Kaw reservation. At about the age of fourteen, he moved to Topeka and lived with paternal grandparents while attending high school. After graduation, he read for the law and opened a practice in the city. Before long he was a successful criminal attorney and active in the Republican Party in Kansas. During these years he was an active supporter of the Kansas law prohibiting the sale of alcoholic beverages.

III

Curtis began his national political career in 1892 with a successful run for Congress. He was a conservative Republican running against the liberal Populist, James Weaver. By this time, Curtis had established himself as an effective vote-getter: always smiling, shaking hands, friendly in demeanor. Even if one disagreed with his ideas, he would invariably like him. One such person reported at the time that his smile and handshake and friendly talk "could persuade a stone statue of his sincerity."

Accompanying his outgoing and engaging personality, Curtis always employed a "common touch." He wore shabby-looking clothes and in all respects tried to be just one of the "common folk." But this was how he got votes, not how he accomplished his conservative political agenda. For that, he was the ultimate behind-the-scenes political operative, working out of public view in the corridors of government and within the party organization.

While he was in the Senate, for example, his colleague, William Borah of Idaho, called him "a great reconciler, a walking political encyclopedia and one of the greatest political poker players in America." In December, 1926, *Time* magazine put him on its cover and wrote in an article: "It is in the party caucuses, in the committee rooms, in the cloakrooms that he patches up troubles and puts through legislation."

During his six terms in Congress, Curtis was, not surprisingly, especially active in developing legislation affecting Native Americans. As a member of the House Committee on Indian Affairs, he promoted rights for Native Americans as individual citizens not as members of a tribe. In fact, he went so far in the law named for him, the Curtis Act, as to abolish all tribal courts. This, of course, did not win him many friends among Native American tribal leaders.

While in Congress. Curtis was usually a supporter of the policies of President Coolidge, especially his opposition to government support for the economy and to an aggressive foreign policy. Disengagement of government from most areas of public life was their shared philosophy. For his loyalty, Curtis expected to be rewarded with a top-level appointment in Coolidge's administration. The Republican Convention of 1928 chose not to nominate Coolidge for a second term and selected Herbert Hoover instead. Fortunately for Curtis' expectations, Hoover chose him as his running mate and they won the general election in a landslide vote.

IV

By the time he settled into his vice presidential office in Washington, Curtis was a widower. His half-sister, "Dolly" Gann, moved in with him and assumed the role of hostess. The pair entertained lavishly, often in their ten-room suite at the Mayflower Hotel.

As vice president, Charles regularly attended cabinet meetings even though his advice on matters of policy was rarely offered or sought by the president. For the most part, he supported Hoover's conservative Republican agenda, especially regarding the need for high protective tariffs to keep out foreign competition in the economy. He was also with Hoover on the most controversial issue of the day—prohibition of alcoholic beverages. He spoke out frequently on the effects of the growing economic depression. "Nothing really to worry about," was his message. Hard times come and go and this depression will be gone in short order.

When Franklin Roosevelt and the Democrats defeated the Hoover-Curtis ticket in a landslide 1932 victory, no one was more surprised than Curtis. How could the voters have no heeded his advice that "all would soon be well?"

V

Curtis remained in Washington practicing law during the early years of FDR's presidency as the economic depression steadily worsened. In February, 1936, he died of a heart attack at the age of seventy-seven.

Nothing of note remains as a permanent reminder of his legacy—only a few portrayals by actors in minor background parts in movies featuring more memorable figures as, for example the 1951 movie, *Jim Thorpe—All American* in which he is portrayed opening the 1932 Olympic Games.

JOHN NANCE GARNER
(Library of Congress)

JOHN NANCE GARNER
(1868-1967)
1933-1941
Cactus Jack and his Bucket of Warm P—

I

THE FIRST OF FRANKLIN D. Roosevelt's three vice presidents, a man who was at first a supporter and later an opponent, James Nance Garner has the distinction of being the longest living vice president at 98 years of age.

Not many other distinctions remain as a legacy of this important public figure who deserves major credit for much of F.D.R.'s New Deal programs and was, in his day, one of the most popular leaders in the country. Unless, that is, one wishes to include among his memorable deeds the comment he made about the vice presidency shortly after leaving that esteemed post. This office, he said "is not worth a bucket of warm p—-."

II

John Nance Garner was born in a log cabin in eastern Texas on November 22, 1868. Later. his father, John Nance Garner III, became a successful cotton grower and society leader whose beautiful home was

139

a social center with many dinner parties for important people in that part of Texas.

After attending local schools, John entered the University of Tennessee in 1885 but remained for only a year. He withdrew because of a number of serious medical problems including poor vision and a weak respiratory system. Then he read law for a time before opening a practice in Uvalde, Texas in 1890. Shortly thereafter, he ran for county judge and defeated his opponent, Marietta Rheimer, whom he married a few years later.

III

Elected to the Texas House of Representatives in 1898, Garner became popular there, probably best remembered for his role in the debate over what to name the State flower. He was with those who favored the prickly pear cactus. Soon everyone was calling him "Cactus Jack," a name that stuck with him for the rest of his life—and beyond.

In 1903, at age thirty-four, John ran for a seat in the U.S. House of Representatives. The popular East Texan won easily. Thus began a thirty-year career in Congress, with his wife serving as his private secretary for all fourteen terms. Before his distinguished career in Congress was over, he would serve as Minority Leader, Majority Leader, Chair of the powerful Ways and Means Committee, Majority Whip and Speaker of the House.

During his years in congress, Garner supported a graduated income tax rather than the flat tax favored by wealthy conservative Republicans. He also opposed the high tariffs designed to protect American business. With these acts, he identified himself as a progressive Democrat. He was also opposed to all slavery and the Klu Klux Klan (KKK) burned a cross on his lawn.

Garner was also an opponent of Prohibition. While in the House, he established and hosted what he called "the board of education"—a place where members could gather and enjoy a drink together. He called this activity "a blow for liberty."

By 1932 he was so well-known and celebrated throughout the country that he could have been a serious contender for the Democratic presidential nomination. In early balloting at the Party Convention, he failed to garner enough votes to be a likely winner and so gave his delegates to FDR who rewarded him by making him his vice presidential running mate. They won the general election in a landslide victory.

IV

As vice president, Garner was typically disparaging of the office. However, unlike many others in that post, he used the office effectively to win friends for himself and supporters for his policies. He was an enormous aid to FDR during their early years together, largely out of loyalty to the president rather than approval of his ideas for the country. Later, during their second term together, he began to oppose much of FDR's "New Deal" program. He especially disliked the new Social Security legislation and laws designed to support labor unions and their right to strike. These and similar parts of the New Deal he described as "plain damn foolishness."

Garner's first open break with FDR came in 1936 when they disagreed publically over a sit-down strike by the Auto Workers Union. The president avidly supported the strike whereas Garner just as firmly opposed it. His argument was that the workers were simply "taking over property" that belonged to someone else.

An even more serious rift occurred over the president's efforts to expand the size of the Supreme Court and other federal courts. His motive, obvious to most at the time, was to appoint new judges who would support his New Deal programs when faced with challenges in the courts. This effort has been commonly referred to as his "packing the courts" scheme. The problem FDR faced in carrying out his plan was that Congress and not the president had the constitutional power to reorganize the court system. To resolve this issue he appointed his vice president to work out some sort of compromise with Congress.

Garner was successful in reaching an agreement with Congress whereby there would be no increase in the size of the courts but Congress would approve most of FDR's New Deal proposals. This success in stopping the court packing scheme, along with early actions opposing federal government "interference" in the economy, established Garner as the leader of the conservative wing of the Democratic Party.

V

In 1940, Garner ran against FDR for the presidential nomination but lost overwhelmingly. Surprised and depressed by the loss, he left Washington and returned to his home in Uvalde, Texas. There he lived quietly for twenty-seven years, enjoying his family, managing his extensive real estate holdings and doing some fishing. The longest-lived vice president in history, he died in 1967 at age ninety-eight—just three months short of his ninety-ninth birthday.

There is not much to remind one of Garner's remarkable career despite the fact that one historian has recently described him as "the most powerful Vice President in the history of the United States." There are a few memorials in and around his hometown of Uvalde Texas but otherwise he will probably always be best remembered, if at all, by his timeless description of the vice presidency—something to do with "piss."

Sorry!

HENRY AGARD WALLACE
(Library of Congress)

HENRY A. WALLACE
(1888-1965)
1941-1945
"The Century of the Common Man"

I

ONE OF THE MOST controversial vice presidents, Henry A. Wallace, was widely thought to be a communist during the time of virulent anti-communism marked by Senator Joseph McCarthy's infamous "witch hunts."

In addition to being an outspoken left-leaning politician, Wallace was an important part of the international spiritualist movement of the early twentieth century. After examining Buddhism, Hinduism and astrology, he became a leader in the movement called "theosophy" or the "wisdom religion." This, it seemed to him, nicely combined his interests in science and religious spiritualism.

As a scientist, Wallace's major work was in agricultural. His experiments in breeding hybrid corn were highly successful, leading to an increase in corn production worldwide—as far away as China. His long political career included service as Secretary of Agriculture and Vice President under FDR and Secretary of Commerce during the presidency of Harry Truman.

II

Henry A. Wallace was born on October 7, 1888 on a farm in New Orient, Iowa. He earned his B.S. degree in animal husbandry from Iowa State University in 1910 and then worked for nearly fifteen years as an editor for the family-owned periodical, *Wallace Farmer.* His father, Henry C. Wallace, had been Secretary of Agriculture under President Warren Harding in the early twenties and the Wallace family generally was known throughout the mid-west as well-grounded in agricultural science.

In hundreds of articles written in the *Wallace Farmer*, Henry A. displayed his commitment to a communal rather than a highly individualistic basis for "democracy." Again and again, he extolled what he variously described as "shared abundance," cooperation," and "communal living." Little wonder that as a young man he was already displaying commitment to what many Americans of the day would simply call "communism," or at least "socialism"—neither of which was widely acceptable in the U.S. during most of the twentieth century.

In 1914, at the age of twenty-four, Wallace married Ilo Browne of Indianola, Iowa. The couple was married for over fifty years and had three children. Ilo was a supportive mate, always involved in her husband's career. When, for example, he was loudly booed by the audience after his speech at the Democratic Party Convention in 1940, she was standing next to him on the platform.

Also, while still a young man, Wallace began exploring various "religious" groups to see where he might find an elaboration of his growing sense of an inner spiritual power which seemed to him to be increasingly directing his ideas and behavior. For a time, he studied and then became part of a Buddhist community and found this helpful as an affirmation of the importance of rising above the suffering of life by seeking enlightenment at a higher level of consciousness. He also studied Hinduism for a time. But it was astrology—hardly a religion, many would say, where he discovered a realm of experience clearly above this mortal world, a realm he thought attainable by a heightened "spiritual" awareness.

Insofar as the outward expression of his "religious" life was concerned, Wallace attended a variety of Protestant churches, especially the Presbyterian Church in which he had been raised as a child. In the latter years of his life, he became an Episcopalian—a denomination known for its broad "via media" which seemed to welcome a large variety of individual interpretations of a basic Christian faith.

III

In 1933, Wallace's career in national government service began when FDR appointed him as his first Secretary of Agriculture—a position which, as we have noted, his father had held about a decade earlier. Almost at once, Henry displayed the aggressive and controversial style that would mark his career in public life when he ordered the slaughter of all baby pigs and the plowing under of all corn crops. His motive was to reduce supply, increase prices and thereby improve the income of farmers. But to take such action during an economic depression when tens of thousands of people were existing on near-starvation diets was hardly acceptable to the average citizen.

The pig-slaughter and corn-destruction programs were part of the Agricultural Adjustment Act (AAA) of 1933 which Wallace had designed and got though Congress. In 1936, the Supreme Court declared this law unconstitutional as an invalid interference by the federal government in state government prerogatives. Wallace then wrote the major provisions of the legislation in such a way as to get them passed as separate laws which were constitutional. In this new form, much of the agricultural policy he designed remains in force to the present day. The historian, Arthur Schlesinger, Jr., has called Wallace the "best Secretary of Agriculture this country ever had."

IV

When FDR ran for his third term in the White House in 1940, he chose Wallace as his vice presidential running mate. With such a progressive candidate FDR hoped to balance his previously strong support for the conservative wing of his Democratic Party. However, Wallace was not a popular choice among most of the convention delegates who were, of course, the leaders of the Party. When he rose to give his acceptance speech, he was greeted by prolonged hisses, hoots, boos and associated profanities. So intense and prolonged was this expression of hostility toward her husband that Ilo wept openly while standing on the stage beside him.

In the vote that followed, it soon appeared that Wallace would be rejected as the Party candidate; whereupon, FDR threatened to withdraw his own candidacy if Wallace were not chosen. Even at that, Wallace won the nomination by only a very small majority. During the general election campaign, Henry was vicious in his attacks on the Republicans, accusing them of being pro-Hitler in what he foresaw as the coming war with Nazi Germany. (He had apparently already decided that we should welcome his new friends in .Russia as our allies in that conflict.)

Wallace's first assignment as vice president was to head a delegation to Mexico in an effort to negotiate a treaty to end that Country's seizure of U.S. oil companies there. He had only moderate success in this endeavor but did manage to soothe tensions and establish a more cordial atmosphere for on-going negotiations. His amiable personality proved once again to be his greatest asset. This experience in Mexico would make him a life-long advocate of improved hemispheric relations.

Insofar as his single constitutional responsibility was concerned, Wallace was an excellent presiding officer in the Senate. His office was a virtual library, filled with the favorite books of this consummate intellectual. In 1942, Wallace gave the most famous and controversial of his many speeches. He called it, *The Price of Free World Victory* and in it he coined the phrase that would remain his mantra for generations to come: "The Century of the common man." A year later he wrote a book with this title. The work was widely criticized as being pro-socialist, and even communist by leading Republicans and Democrats alike, as well as by such leaders overseas as English Prime Minister, Sir Winston Churchill.

Despite his being so widely regarded as too progressive by so many Americans, FDR wanted him as part of his reelection bid in 1944. Partly, this was because Wallace had recently received a 65% approval rating among the general public in a national Gallop Poll; partly, it was because FDR wanted to demonstrate that, despite some of his recent policy decisions, he remained a true liberal himself.

But then Wallace did something that ruined his chances for high elective office. He confirmed suspicions that he was pro-communist by undertaking an extended trip to Russia and Asia. He met personally with such figures as Vyacheslav Molotov. He also became fluent in the Russian language and traveled throughout the country, through Siberia and finally into communist China. There would never be much doubt, after that, that he was favorably disposed to communism as a system of government.

By the time Wallace returned home, FDR had changed his mind about him, largely due to pressure from conservative party leaders, especially in the South. Harry Truman was chosen to run with FDR. Although not well known in the country at large, the Missouri Senator was at least viewed as a conservative Democrat who was strongly opposed to Soviet Communism.

V

Following his re-election to a fourth term, FDR appointed Wallace Secretary of Commerce. After Roosevelt's death in 1945, he remained in this post for about a year-and-a-half under President Harry Truman. The two had strong disagreements, some of them publically expressed, over policies toward the Soviet Union. Truman fired Wallace from his Commerce post in September of 1946.

Wallace then began a short career as editor of the *New Republic*. In this role he continued strong attacks on Truman, calling the so-called "Truman Doctrine" of 1948, which launched a period of aggressive foreign policy, the beginning of "a century of fear" for the U.S. and the world.

In 1948, Wallace made one last bid for high public office—this time for the presidency itself. He ran on the Progressive Party ticket, calling for an end to the Truman Doctrine and the "cold war." He also spoke out in favor of civil rights for African Americans and universal government-supported health care. In this campaign he was publicly endorsed by the U.S. Communist Party and received less than three percent of the popular vote.

Returning to his farm in upstate New York shortly after his election defeat, Wallace resumed his passion for experimental agriculture. His work developing new strains of popular flowers, hybrid corn and chickens capable of laying more eggs won him world-wide acclaim as they were adopted in countries around the globe.

In 1950, Wallace did a complete about-face politically when he wrote a book entitled *Where I Was Wrong*. In this work he renounced his earlier pro-Soviet positions and said he was now a confirmed anti-communist. He also endorsed the election of Republican Dwight Eisenhower as president.

In November, 1965, Wallace died of amystropic lateral sclerosis, popularly know as Lou Gerhrig's disease. He had suffered with this sickness for about a year after one of his many trips to South America. He was seventy-seven years old.

Like so many of his vice presidential compatriots, Wallace is little remembered today—save for his pro-communist activities and a few minor memorials. In 2012, for example, Oliver Stone did a television documentary entitled *Roosevelt, Truman and Wallace*. Less memorable, perhaps, is the so-called "Wallace melon," the name given in China to one of his agricultural products which is still consumed in that country.

ALBEN W. BARKLEY
(Library of Congress)

Alben W. Barkley
(1877-1956)
1949-1953
The Most Fascinating American??

I

OUR THIRTY-FIFTH VICE PRESIDENT, Alben W. Barkley, was an aggressive, progressive, liberal Democrat who served in Congress for nearly four decades during the presidencies of Woodrow Wilson, Warren Harding, Calvin Coolidge and Franklin Roosevelt, before becoming a vice president under Harry Truman in 1949.

Barkley had close and important and, for the most part, cordial relations with all of the presidents during his long tenure in Congress. He was a person of enormous personal charm as well as an effective speaker. Among his more controversial positions as a public official was his avid support of an amendment to the Constitution outlawing the consumption of alcoholic beverages. He was also one of the relatively few vice presidents up to his time who thought the office to be an important one. He did all that he could to improve its stature in the federal government.

II

Alben Barkley was a true "rags-to-riches," "log-cabin" vice president. Born in rural Kentucky on November 24, 1877, he was raised in a poor subsistenc-level environment, living in a small log cabin while his father tried, usually without much success, to make a living as a tenant farmer raising tobacco—the cheap kind used for chewing, not smoking. As a boy, Alben sometimes worked on the farm with his father but was otherwise at home helping raise his younger brother and sisters. At home, Alben endured a rigid puritan-style upbringing. Alcohol , card- playing, music, dancing and all such "immoral" frivolities were forbidden in this strict Presbyterian household.

In 1891, the poor struggling family moved to Clinton, Kentucky so that Alben, who had previously attended a few local "common schools" on a part-time basis, could enroll in Marvin College—a preparatory school owned and run by the Methodist Church. He received his degree from Marvin in 1897. Now, under the somewhat more permissive influence of Methodism, he chose law as a career rather than the ministry which his father had planned for him.

Alben then moved to Atlanta, Georgia and entered another Methodist school, Emory College, to begin his pre-law studies. Lack of funds, however, forced him to leave after only a year and return to Marvin College to work as a teacher. Meanwhile, he continued to read for the bar exam which he passed in 1901. The following year he burnished his legal education a bit by attending the University of Virginia Law School for a few months.

Returning to Paducah, Alben became very active in the local social life, joining such groups as Wooden Sons of the World, Benevolent and Protective Order of Elks and Independent Order of Odd Fellows— known more simply and popularly as Woodsmen, Elks and Odd Fellows. He also became a leader in the local Methodist Church, preaching and giving speeches on religious and political subjects all over that part of Kentucky.

In 1903, Barkley married a local Paducah woman, Dorothy Bower. The couple enjoyed a long and mutually supportive relationship. They had three children between 1906 and 1911—one boy (David) and two girls (Marion and Laura). Dorothy died of a heart disease in 1947 and Alben was remarried two years later to Jane Hadley, a lively, attractive lady from St. Louis with whom he had become completely infatuated shortly after Dorothy's death.

III

Barkley first entered politics in 1905 when he won election as County Attorney. He ran an energetic campaign, displaying himself as a friendly, outgoing personality. Soon he had a state-wide reputation as a political figure of ability and great charm. He easily won election as a county judge in 1907.

Within just a few years, Barkley set his sights on a national political office. In 1912, he ran for and won a seat in the U.S. House of Representatives, running as a self-proclaimed "liberal." In those days, this meant that he favored lowering so-called "restrictive" tariffs which, as he saw it, only helped wealthy corporations by keeping out competitive foreign goods. He also favored aggressive use of the Interstate Commerce Commission to regulate and thereby "improve" many parts of the economy, especially railroads. In addition, he vigorously opposed using children as "cheap labor." For these and similar positions, he was branded a "Socialist."

In the same year that Barkley was first elected to Congress, Woodrow Wilson was elected President. The two had much in common and supported one another, especially regards the Clayton Anti-trust Act of 1914 and U.S. neutrality in World War I. Barkley was also strongly opposed to alcohol consumption and became an advocate of a Prohibition Amendment to the Constitution.

In the 1920s, when Warren Harding was President, Barkley supported him in a few matters like the creation of the Veterans Bureau but generally found him too pro-business and generally conservative for his taste. In 1922, he said of Harding's so-called "Return to Normalcy" program that if this worked "then in God's name let us have Abnormalcy."

After completing four terms in the House, Barkley ran for Governor of Kentucky in 1923. He lost in the Democratic primary by a close vote. Four years later, he ran for a seat in the U.S. Senate and won. Before long he was a strong supporter of Franklin Roosevelt and his "New Deal" programs to counteract the devastating effects of the economic depression of the 1930s and '40s.

Barkley was a great help in getting FDR's programs through the Senate, especially during his time as Majority Leader beginning in 1937. He even tried to help the president with his notorious "court-packing" which was a scheme designed to assure new federal judges who would be favorable to New Deal legislation when challenged in the courts. Barkley was known in these years of his career in Congress as "Mr. Democrat." He was the most sought-after political speaker in the country and *Look Magazine* called him "the most fascinating American."

IV

In 1948, President Harry Truman picked Barkley to be his running mate. Despite his ostensibly high regard for the potential of the office, Barkley confided a different view to a friend at the time.

> There once was a man who had two sons. Both boys showed great promise early in life. But the elder son went to sea and the younger was elected vice president and neither has been heard of since.

Clearly this was not what Barley intended for himself as vice president: "never to be heard of again." Before long he was Truman's main spokesman, travelling extensively and giving countless speeches in support of Truman's policies.

By this time, his wife, Dorothy had died and, as previously noted, almost at once he fell passionately in love with an attractive St. Louis socialite and attorney, Jane Hadley, while she was visiting in Paducah. Because she lived so far away, Alben had to conduct a "cross-country" romance, travelling again and again by plane to be with her. The entire country followed this back-and –forth courtship with fascination until the couple was finally married in November, 1949.

Truman appreciated Barkley's help in Congress and admired his accomplishments so much that, with much ceremony, he came in person to the Senate floor in 1951 and presented Barkely a gavel made of the ancient timber used long ago in the construction of the White House.

V

In 1952, Barkley considered a run for the presidency. He was seventy-four years old and had failing eye sight and recurring heart problems. Generally considered by most potential supporters as too old and infirm to be president, he reluctantly returned to Paducah and wrote his memoirs.

Remarkably, despite his infirmities he ran again for the Senate in 1954 and won. Two years later, just after giving yet another of his countless speeches—this one at Washington and Lee University in Virginia, he dropped dead on the platform. He was seventy-eight years old.

There are a few notable memorials to Alben Barkley. These include Barkley Lake and Dam on the Columbia River, Barkley Regional Airport in Paducah and the Alben Barkley Distinguished Chair of Political Science at Emory University. (Although he had attended Emory for only a year, the university awarded him an Honorary Doctorate of Laws in 1949 when he began his term as vice president.)

HUBERT H. HUMPHREY, JR.
(Library of Congress)

HUBERT H. HUMPHREY
(1911-1978)
1965-1969
The Happy Warrior

I

FEW VICE PRESIDENTS HAVE been such prominent figures in the public life of the country as Hubert H. Humphrey. Although variously acclaimed and disliked by large segments of the population and among historians, few doubt that during the middle decades of the twentieth century he was a dominant political personality. So well known is he that one of my friends actually insisted that Humphrey had been president for at least one term in the '60's or '70's—admitedly my friends, like me, are all in our seventies and eighties and nearing senility!

In fact, Humphrey did try on four different occasions for the Democratic presidential nomination—and did so with so much campaign hoopla and press attention that one might think that, on at least one occasion he would make it. In fact, he did achieve the nomination but then lost the general election on his third attempt. He was also a U.S. Senator for two terms. During that time he was responsible for notable achievements including being one of the founders of both the Americans for Democratic Action (ADA) and the Farm Labor Party of Minnesota and also the author of the historic Civil Rights Act of 1964.

However, during his Senate career Hubert exhibited an inconsistency of behavior that hurt his political ambitions for higher office. Many, even among fellow liberals in his own Party, accused him of dishonesty and hypocrisy—a man who cared for nothing so much as his own political survival. Like him or not, Humphrey was one of the most colorful political figures of the mid-twentieth century—outspoken lively, controversial and constantly in the public eye.

II

Hubert Humphrey was born in May, 1911 in Wallace, South Dakota and grew up in Doland, a small village of fewer than a thousand inhabitants, also in South Dakota. His father, Hubert, Sr., was a local druggist who served for a time as mayor of the town. His mother, Regnild Sannes, was a Norwegian who had come to this country as a young woman. After Hubert graduated from the local high school, the family moved to Huron, a much larger city in the State which offered better opportunities for enlarging their pharmaceutical business.

In 1930, Hubert attended the University of Minnesota for about a year before leaving to help his father in his expanding drugstore business. Within a few years, the Humphrey Drug Company was a prosperous enterprise and Hubert returned to the University to receive his degree in political science with Phi Beta Kappa honors. In 1939 he earned his MA degree while serving as a part-time instructor in political science.

Meanwhile, while still working in the family business in Huron in 1936, Humphrey had married Muriel Buck, a professional bookkeeper who had recently graduated from Huron College. The couple was married for the rest of their lives—some forty-two years. They had four children: one girl and three boys.

When World War II broke out in the early 1940s, Hubert tried to enlist but was rejected because of a hernia ailment. During the war, he was active in a number of national and state organizations supporting the war effort, including service as Assistant Director of the War Manpower Commission, and leadership posts in the Works Progress Association (WPA) and the Minnesota Manpower Commission. He was also one of the founders of Americans for Democratic Action (ADA), a liberal, anti-communist organization and, for a short period during the war, he was a professor of political science at Macalester College in St. Paul, Minnesota.

III

Humphrey's first try for elective office was also during the war years when he ran for Mayor of Minneapolis in 1943. He lost this election although he performed well enough in the campaign to garner forty-seven percent of the popular vote. He ran again both in 1945 and 1947, winning both times.

As mayor, Humphrey displayed a vigorous, outgoing, aggressive style. His goal was, as he put it, "to clean up the city." Minneapolis was, indeed, in those days known as one of the most corrupt and crime-ridden places in the country. Gambling, prostitution, anti-semitism, racism and police corruption were all rampant. With great persistence and ability to garner public support with his powerful yet friendly personality, Humphrey succeeded and was soon recognized throughout the country as the "great reformer."

At the 1948 Democratic Convention, Humphrey gave one of the earliest of the "great" speeches of his career. The delegates were sharply divided between liberals and conservatives on such issues as whether or not to end public school segregation and discrimination in hiring by means of national legislation and court action. President Truman tried to keep what he called these contentious "states'-rights" issues out of Convention debate. But Humphrey rose to speak in favor of progressive action on both fronts:

To those who say …this civil-rights program is an infringement on States' rights, I say this: the time has arrived for the Democratic Party to get out of the shadow of States' rights and walk forthrightly into the bright sunshine of human rights.

The Convention then approved the civil rights plank in its platform by a close vote: 651-582. Thereupon, many Southern delegates stormed out of the hall. It was a dramatic episode. Even so, Truman defeated Republican candidate, Governor Thomas Dewey of New York in the general election by a large margin. Black voters turned out in record numbers to support him and help overcome the loss of most Southern White votes.

In 1948, 1954 and 1960 Humphrey was elected to the U.S. Senate—the first Democrat to serve in that body from Minnesota since the Civil War. During his third term, he was elected to fill the powerful position of Minority Whip.

While in the Senate, he favored all civil rights legislation as well as humanitarian foreign aid, food stamps for the poor and strict military arms control. His most notable achievement was the historic Civil Rights Act of 1964, enacted during his final year as a Senator.

Throughout his long tenure in the Senate, Hubert was well regarded by his colleagues—even many who disagreed with his policies—for his integrity, eloquence and friendly rapport with fellow senators. It was at this time that the phrase "The Happy Warrior" came into wide use to characterize his charismatic leadership style.

Despite his accomplishments in the Senate, Humphrey nevertheless came to be highly criticized toward the end of his service there by many of his colleagues for what they regarded as his inconsistent and even duplicitous behavior—not really a leader who was well-informed, thoughtful and adhered to his firmly held convictions. Especially note worthy in this regard, was what was seen as his failure to oppose Senator Joseph McCarthy's virulent anti-communism which was resulting in the harassment and even punishment of fellow liberals. They were viewed as only exercising their rights to free speech. One of his own personal assistants later wrote that Hubert was:

> Nothing but a whirling dervish who absorbed things fantastically quick, but the idea of Humphrey reading a book or sitting down seriously to think about the implications of what he was doing is hard to imagine.

Humphrey made his first run for the presidential nomination in 1952 as a Minnesota "favorite son" and lost overwhelmingly. He tried again in 1960 and fared no better, losing the nomination this time to John Kennedy. (This was a nasty campaign in which Kennedy raised the issue of Hubert's lack of service in World War II, implying that he had been a draft dodger. Kennedy did this probably to distract public attention from the overriding issue of his being a Roman Catholic.)

Between these two presidential bids, Humphrey tried for the vice presidency in 1956. He had been led to believe that the likely presidential candidate, Governor Adlai Stevenson of Illinois, wanted him as his running mate. At the proverbial eleventh hour, however, Stevenson selected Senator Estes Kefauver from among a host of aspirants.

IV

In 1964, Humphrey was finally successful in achieving the Democratic Party vice presidential nomination, running on the ticket with Lyndon Johnson who had assumed the presidency a year earlier after the death of John Kennedy and was now running for the office in his own right. Hubert's principal competition was Senator Eugene McCarthy, a fellow Minnesota Senator with a liberal record to match his own. Throughout the nomination process, LBJ "toyed" with both men leading each to believe that he was his choice. In the end, he picked Humphrey, apparently deciding that he would be the more loyal to him of the two.

The Johnson-Humphrey ticket defeated Republican Barry Goldwater overwhelmingly in the general election with Humphrey playing the key role in the campaign for all of the Democratic ticket. He made effective speeches throughout the country, attacking Goldwater for being opposed both to civil rights and large tax cuts for the lower and middle classes. In his campaign speeches, Humphrey said that many Republicans had voted earlier for each of these progressive policies—"But not Senator Goldwater." He repeated this refrain again and again. The voters loved it.

As vice president, Humphrey continued his advocacy of civil rights and social welfare programs which seemed generally to be in keeping with LBJ's own positions. Then he made an enormous mistake by opposing the war in Vietnam, especially the bombing of North Vietnam which killed thousands of civilians. This position was in keeping with his general approach to foreign policy and doubtless pleased his fellow liberals in and out of government. But LBJ was not pleased and thereafter treated him coldly and cut him off from his inner circle of advisors. Humphrey then completely reversed himself and endorsed the very war he had been condemning. This reversal led to his being shunned by most of his liberal friends and supporters who accused him of being a hypocrite and liar. The entertainer, Tom Lehrer, wrote and sang a satirical ditty about Humphrey:

> Whatever became of Hubert? Has anyone heard a thing? Once he shone on his own, now he sits home alone and waits for the phone to ring. Once a fiery liberal spirit ah, but now when he speaks he must clear it.

In 1968, Humphrey made yet another bid for the presidency, this time running against Richard Nixon. Because of Nixon's general unpopularity with the public at the time, Humphrey did surprisingly well in the popular vote, losing by only about one percent, though the margin in the Electoral College was much larger: 301-196. Hindering Humphrey's chances in the election was his association with Lyndon Johnson, who by this time was almost as poorly regarded by many in the public as Nixon. Also his own failure to have spoken out against the killing by police of anti-war protestors, especially during the recent

"Chicago Riots," hurt his cause, as did the assassination of both Martin Luther King, Jr. and Robert Kennedy during the election campaign itself.

V

During his retirement years, Humphrey taught for a time at Macalester College in Minnesota. Then, in 1970, unbelievably, he ran for high office yet again—this time for a seat in the U.S. Senate. He won the election and did so for yet another term in 1976. When near death, he tried again for the presidency. By this time, he was suffering severely from bladder cancer and withdrew early in the nominating process in favor of Jimmy Carter.

On January 13, 1979, Humphrey died of cancer at home. His wife, Muriel, was appointed at once by Minnesota Governor Rudy Perpich to replace him in the Senate until an election to fill his seat could be held.

Hubert Humphrey's primary legacy is as a nearly unforgettable political personality during the middle decades of the twentieth century. His engaging, assertive but always pleasant and charming personality, and his perennial candidacy for the presidency have made him a truly memorable figure. Whether or not always well informed on the details of issues facing the country, his winning persona usually carried the day for him. His legacy for all presidential aspirants: "just keep trying"—though he never made it himself.

In terms of physical memorials, Humphrey has more than most of his fellow vice presidents to date. There are about fifteen buildings in his honor—mostly in Minnesota but ranging all over the country from Florida to California. These include statues, airports, stadiums, bridges, schools and hospitals. The most notable is the Hubert Humphrey Building in Washington, D.C, which is the headquarters for the U. S. Department of Health and Human Services.

SPIRO T. AGNEW
(Library of Congress)

SPIRO AGNEW
(1918-1996)
1969-1973
Spiro Who???

I

AMONG OUR LARGELY FORGOTTEN vice presidents, Spiro Agnew is one who many may remember but probably wish they didn't. His political career was so marked by corruption, bribery and even theft that he has left a stain on the history of this high office—the only vice president forced to resign the office because of his outrageous and illegal behavior.

As a life-long Republican living in the predominantly Democratic State of Maryland and desiring high public office there, Agnew resorted often to inconsistent—some would say duplicitous behavior. His election as governor in 1966 was the result of overwhelming support from Black voters who approved his opposition to racial segregation. But later, as we shall see, when it suited his political purposes he turned against the African-Americans accusing them of inciting dangerous and needless disturbances throughout the state.

II

The first Greek-American to be vice president, Spiro Agnew was born in Baltimore, Maryland in November, 1918. His father, Theodore, was a Greek immigrant and his mother, Margaret Pollard, was a widow from Virginia. Spiro was the couple's only child.

After attending local schools during his boyhood, Spiro enrolled at Johns Hopkins University in 1937 to major in chemistry. He was drafted into the army in 1941 before completing his degree and was soon serving in Europe as an officer in the Tenth Armored Division. For his bravery in battles in Germany and France, he was awarded the Bronze Star. While still in Europe in 1942, he married Elinor Judefind ("Judy"). The couple was to have four children—a boy and three girls.

Back home in Baltimore after the war, Agnew entered the University of Baltimore Law School as a part-time student while working at a variety of jobs in the city. In 1949, he passed the bar exam and opened a practice. Before long, he was casting about for some way to get into State politics.

III

As a Republican in a predominantly Democratic state, it took Agnew nearly a decade to gain a government position. In 1957, he was appointed a member of the Baltimore County Zoning Appeals Board. In 1962, he made his first bid for elective office when he ran for Baltimore County Executive.

In this campaign, he presented himself as a liberal Republican who opposed the segregationist policies of the Democrat majority party. Although his civil-rights advocacy was limited to little more than opposition to racial discrimination in public places, he won overwhelming support of African-American voters as was elected. (Shortly thereafter, he was, in fact, instrumental in having his modest civil rights proposal enacted into law. It was the first such anti-discrimination law in the country.)

In 1966, Agnew made his bid for the governorship of Maryland. Once again, as a liberal Republican in a Democratic state, he was able to take advantage of a badly divided Democratic Party in which many held extreme segregationist views. He appealed to Blacks who, by this time, were very appreciative of his work on their behalf while serving as County Executive. He won the election handily running against segregationist George Mahoney who used the campaign slogan: "Your home is your castle; protect it." (Black voters had no doubt about just who it was that Mahoney was referring to as being a threat to White homes.)

As Governor, Spiro was decidedly moderate on racial issues. He favored open-housing laws and a few other civil rights proposals but focused his attention largely on other matters such as court reform and anti-pollution measures. Before long his pro-Black positions were being viewed by many as opportunistic. This opinion seemed confirmed when he expressed his negative reaction to riots in Baltimore following the assassination of Martin Luther King, Jr. in the spring of 1968.

He summoned about one hundred African-American leaders to his office and berated them, blaming them for the riots and general disorder they caused in the city. To their faces, he called them: "caterwauling, riot-inciting, burn-down-America types of leaders." He also told them that they should have "publically repudiated" fellow African-Americans who are "all Black racists" and which "thus far you have been unwilling to do."

As this castigation of Black leaders became widely known, conservative Whites in the Republican Party urged Nixon to consider Agnew as his running mate in the 1968 presidential election. After meeting with Spiro, Nixon asked him to make the speech nominating him for president at the upcoming Republican Convention and also asked to run with him in the general election. Agnew readily agreed to both requests.

IV

At the Republican Convention all went as Nixon and Agnew had planned except for one detail—many of the delegates had no idea who was this fellow with the strange name they were being asked to nominate. At one point, they shouted out those timeless words which would become Agnew's political persona to the present day: "SPIRO WHO ???"

Nevertheless, the man with the strange name was nominated and became the principal apologist and campaigner for Nixon against Democratic candidate, Hubert Humphrey. The major issue in the campaign was the unpopular war in Vietnam for which Nixon was seen as largely responsible. The task of taking on opponents to the war was assigned to Agnew who became Nixon's "hatchet man" to destroy all such "traitors."

The likes of Hubert Humphrey himself were quickly branded by Agnew as disloyal to their country. Humphrey was also famously called by Agnew a man who was "soft on communism," a phrase repeated so often that it has been thought to have played a major role in defeating Humphrey's run against Nixon for the presidency.

When Agnew ran again for the vice presidency on Nixon's ticket in 1972, he continued his torrent of abuse toward all who opposed the war in Vietnam, including opposition presidential candidate, George McGovern, who he called "one of the greatest frauds ever to be considered as a presidential candidate by a major American Party." He also accused Humphrey and others of all manner of crimes, using a host of memorable and phrases to characterize them, such as:

"nattering nabobs of negativism"
"pusillanimous pussyfooters"
"effete snobs."

During his years as vice president, Spiro was almost totally cut off from any governing responsibility.. Nixon delegated virtually nothing to him and rarely permitted him even to visit the Oval Office. What the president did allow—and expect—was Agnew's constant speech-making on behalf of the president and his policies. Spiro did as he was bid and in the process became one of the major fund-raisers for Nixon during his time in office.

Having few responsibilities as vice president, Agnew spent much of his tenure engaged in something he truly enjoyed—hob-nobbing (as he surely would have termed such activity) with celebrities. Before long he was spending time with the likes of Frank Sinatra and Bob Hope as well traveling to be with famous people, including government leaders, all over the world. Nixon tolerated all of this, apparently happy to have Agnew out of sight.

V

In late 1973, shortly after election to his second term as vice president, Agnew resigned from the office as part of a deal which kept him out of prison for his illegal acts when governor of Maryland. What Nixon had not known when he asked Agnew to be his running mate in 1968 was that, while serving years before as governor of Maryland, Agnew had committed deeds that would one day destroy his reputation and be a great embarrassment to Nixon. This was a kick-back scheme in which he solicited bribes from major companies in return for awarding them lucrative government contracts. It would later be alleged that he had made himself over $100,000 in these illegal deals. When his notorious behavior was discovered during his vice presidency, Agnew was able to avoid a prison term by resigning his office and paying a $10,000 fine for taxes owed on unreported income. Later, he was sued by Maryland residents for the actual amount he was thought to have taken in bribes, estimated at over $260,000. He eventually paid that amount in 1983.

He was only the second vice president to resign from the office. The first was John C. Calhoun who had a resigned in 1832 for the much more acceptable reason that he wished to accept election to the U.S. Senate by the South Carolina legislature. Upon his resignation, the Twenty-Fifth Amendment to the Constitution, enacted in 1967, was applied for the first time and House Majority Leader, Gerald Ford, became our fortieth vice president.

For his part, Agnew returned to his home in Baltimore and worked for a time as a trade representative for a few luxury home developments. He managed to stay in the public eye—naturally—by another notorious act. This time it was making repeated statements against the State of Israel and U.S. support of that country. His remarks bordered on anti-Semitism. He also published his personal memoir in which he alleged that Nixon had threatened to have him assassinated unless he resigned as vice president.

Agnew died of leukemia in September, 1996 at the age of seventy-seven. There are no significant physical memorials as a legacy but many will long remember his incredibly outlandish behavior as a public official.

NELSON A. ROCKEFELLER
(Library of Congress)

NELSON A. ROCKEFELLER
(1908-1979)
1974-1977
"The Rockefeller Salute"

I

NELSON ROCKEFELLER IS ONE of the most "liberal" Republicans ever to serve as vice president. His record, both as vice president and as long-time governor of New York, is marked by the sort of progressive policies one usually associates with the Democratic Party: civil rights for every type for African-Americans and women; environmental protection and government expenditures for such public works as highways, bridges, and airports. In almost every respect he was a change-oriented official bent on improving the quality of life for everyone.

Rockefeller was also probably the wealthiest person ever to be vice president. What is most noteworthy about his riches is that he did not lavish them on himself but used his money to support the kind of philanthropic causes which supported his broad liberal agenda.

Like so many other vice presidents, Rockefeller truly wanted not that office but the presidency. In fact, he tried three times for the Oval Office—all unsuccessfully. Nevertheless, he treated the number two post with great respect and, unlike many of his predecessors, used it fully to achieve his goals as a policy-maker.

II

Born in Bar Harbor, Maine on July 8, 1908, Nelson was the son of John and Abby Aldrich Rockefeller. He was the descendent of a long line of wealthy ancestors who had made prominent records as leaders in business and public life. His maternal grandfather, for example, was the founder of the Standard Oil Company and a U. S. Senator.

One of six children, Nelson was raised in opulent surroundings, growing up in beautiful homes, attending the best schools and lacking in no creature comforts. Amidst all this wealth, however, his father instilled in him the virtues of thrift, hard work and generosity to those less fortunate. For example, he was given an allowance of only thirty cents a week and could keep only ten cents for his own use. He had to divide the rest between savings and charity.

In 1930, Nelson graduated from Dartmouth College, *cum laude* and with a Phi Beta Kappa key. In the same year, he married Mary Clark ("Tod") who was also from a wealthy and prominent family extending back to early colonial days. The couple was married for thirty-one years and had five children, most of whom became well-known public figures.

After his marriage, Nelson worked for his father in various family businesses, including Chase Bank and the Rockefeller Center. From 1935-1940, he was Chairman of Creole Petroleum, the branch of Standard Oil in Venezuela. That experience launched a life-long interest in Latin American affairs marked, among other things, by his later appointment by Franklin Roosevelt to serve as Coordinator in the Office of Inter-American Affairs (OIAA). In this role, he worked for decades to improve living standards in Latin America and to develop improved relations between the U. S. and governments in that part of the world.

III

In 1944, FDR appointed Rockefeller Assistant Secretary of State and a year later delegate to the United Nations Conference on International Organizations—the group which founded the United Nations. Shortly thereafter, he left government service but returned soon when President Truman made him Chair of the International Development Board in 1950. This was the organization charged with implementing international technical assistance for underdeveloped countries under Truman's Point-Four Program.

Shortly after Dwight Eisenhower was elected president in 1952, he named Rockefeller chair of his Advisory Committee on Government Organization. The purpose of this group was to improve overall efficiency and execution of policy in the executive branch. In this work, as in previous assignments, Nelson performed admirably in accomplishing what he had been assigned to do. Congress, however, failed to approve his program for government reorganization. Undaunted, Eisenhower continued his confidence in Nelson when he asked him, in 1953, to create a cabinet-level Department of Health, Education and Welfare and to serve as its first Secretary. He did so and that branch of the executive remains much as he designed it to the present day.

In 1954, Rockefeller accepted yet another presidential appointment. This time it was as Special Assistant to the President for Foreign Affairs—with particular reference to the growing need to counter the spying activities of the Soviet Union and to develop a national security program to protect the country from the growing Soviet threat.

Leaving government service again in 1956, Rockefeller created the Special Studies Project whose purpose was to study the future of the nation—both its problems and its prospects. The study, funded by his own Rockefeller Brothers Foundation, was directed by Henry Kissinger, who would soon become Nelson's personal confidant, advisor and close friend.

In 1961, the Special Studies Project published its results: *Prospect for America*. Both Eisenhower and, later, President Kennedy, endorsed and implemented parts of the Report, especially those dealing with the need to build up the military in response to the increasing military aggressiveness of the Soviet Union.

Rockefeller began, in the late 1950's, to turn his full attention to New York State when he was elected to the first of four terms as Governor. It was during these years that he truly established himself as a progressive leader committed to improving all aspects of the lives of the people. Among many other accomplishments, he greatly expanded the reach of education by making New York State University the largest state system in the country with seventy-two separate campuses. He also, as previously noted, led the movement in the State to outlaw virtually every form of racial and gender discrimination, whether in hiring practices, housing availability or access to all public facilities including restaurants, stores, and transportation. Rarely had there been such a sweeping agenda to eliminate discrimination.

While serving as governor, Nelson continued his interest and involvement in Latin-American affairs. In 1969, President Nixon sent him on a mission to visit some twenty countries and make recommendations to him on future policies toward them and the region as a whole. Rockefeller once again, did as bid and made a widely acclaimed report to the president. Nixon, however, took virtually no actions to implement Nelson's recommendations.

Some disapproval of Rockefeller's generally applauded behavior began as early as 1962 when he was still Governor of New York. This occurred when he divorced his popular wife, Tod, and married Margaret "Happy" Murphy, a divorcee with four children. Serious doubts about his leadership abilities began to arise in 1971 during the Attica, New York prison riots. When prisoners captured guards and visitors and held them hostage, Rockefeller ordered an attack which resulted in the killing of thirty-nine inmates and hostages. This was the largest loss of life during such an event in U. S. history. The fact that the governor had never come to the prison in person to try to negotiate with the prisoners but merely ordered an attack resulting in such a massacre led to a marked decline in his popularity.

In 1973, Rockefeller began to look beyond his State for an outlet for his talents when he established his Commission on Critical Choices for Americans. He selected forty-two prominent citizens to serve on the Commission. Little was done at the time to implement the impressive and far-reaching recommendations of the Commission's Report but it did repair some of Rockefeller's reputation and found later expression in his work as vice-president while serving on the Energy Independence Authority (EIA) and other agencies with which he worked under President Ford.

IV

By the time Rockefeller ran for the vice presidency in 1974, he had already sought the Republican nomination for president on three different occasions: the first in 1960 when he lost to Richard Nixon; the second in 1964 when Barry Goldwater was the Party's choice; the third in 1968 when Nixon won both the nomination and the general election.

His route to the vice presidency proved to be difficult. When Gerald Ford became president, following Nixon's resignation in 1974, he asked Congress to elect Rockefeller as vice president. Congress complied but not before subjecting Nelson to a grueling investigation of his finances. They were especially concerned about large investments he had in companies currently doing business with the government. Would this not create a serious conflict of interest?

In response, Rockefeller assured the Committee that he was not so wealthy as they imagined and that, in any event, he held only modest investments in companies like Standard Oil currently doing business with the government. During the hearings, however, his record as Governor of New York was revealed showing that he had, in fact, solicited large bribes from companies in return for contracts with the State—a classic "kick-back" scheme.

Rockefeller replied to these accusations by claiming that there was no lasting harm in what he had done and that his behavior was certainly not illegal. The surprising outcome of the confirmation process was that he was approved by a comfortable margin, probably because President Ford wanted him as his vice president.

What distinguishes Rockefeller's vice presidency, more than anything else, is that he treated the office seriously and with respect and made good use of the opportunities it afforded to make important policy decisions. His intention from the start was to play a major role in all executive-level decisions but he was vigorously opposed by White House Chief of Staff, Donald Rumsfeld, who saw these responsibilities as solely within the authority of the president—and, therefore, himself.

Rumsfeld notwithstanding, Ford did make considerable use of his aggressive vice president. He appointed him to his Commission on Organization of the Government for the Conduct of Foreign Policy and to a number of other study commissions. Once again, Rockefeller found himself limited to making recommendations and not policy. Even the main post he was given, as Chair of the Domestic Council—a group designed to develop and implement policies on energy independence—frustrated him as it turned out to be but one more advisory group. He withdrew from that office in 1975, after less than a year.

During his years as vice president, Rockefeller donated all of his salary to charities: one-half to educational and social welfare programs designed to assist underprivileged urban children and one-half to promote the arts in public schools.

V

When Gerald Ford ran for reelection in 1976, he did not choose Rockefeller as his running mate. By this time, Nelson was far too controversial a figure and so Senator Robert Dole was selected. During the campaign, Rockefeller made many speeches on behalf of the Party ticket. On one such occasion, during a speech at the New York State University campus in Binghamton, Rockefeller was taunted with loud boos from students in the audience. His response became part of

American political legend and, perhaps unfortunately, the one thing for which he is best remembered. He gave his hecklers "the finger"—an obscene gesture whose meaning was lost on no one. Thereafter, this gesture has been known as "The Rockefeller Salute."

In January 1977, at the end of his vice presidency, Rockefeller was publicly honored when President Ford presented him with the Presidential Medal of Freedom. For the final two years of his life, Nelson returned to his art work and published some of it. He also transformed his property in Texas into a jungle filled with wild African animals.

This truly remarkable man died on January 26, 1979 at the age of seventy. At the time of his death, he was in the company of a much younger woman whom he had described as "a research assistant." Uh huh!!

WALTER F. MONDALE
(Library of Congress)

WALTER F. MONDALE
(1928–)
1977-1981
"I'll Raise Your Taxes"

I

WALTER FREDERICK MONDALE WAS the last of the "New Deal" type Democrats to run for president and vice president. By his time, the country in general was more conservative on most issues than it had been for several decades—especially concerning civil-rights initiatives and government spending on social improvements. The trend was clearly toward favoring free enterprise and private initiative in most matters.

Mondale was the first vice president in a long time to make full use of that office although his immediate predecessor, Nelson Rockefeller had certainly begun that trend. The difference here was that in Walter's case the president, Jimmy Carter, wanted him to be a strong vice president—one who was a virtual partner with him in leading the government.

II

At age eighty-five, Mondale is the oldest of the five living ex-vice presidents. Born in Ceylon, Minnesota in 1928, Walter was of Norwegian descent. His father, Theodore, was a Methodist minister and his mother, Claribel Hope, was his father's second wife. As a boy, he was known as "Fritz," a corruption of his middle name, Frederick.

After attending local schools, Mondale entered Macalester College in St. Paul where he quickly became involved in politics. As a freshman, he was active in SDA (Students for Democratic Action) and campaigned for Hubert Humphrey as Mayor of Minneapolis. Later, while still in college, he worked in Humphrey's campaign for the U.S. Senate. In 1948, he dropped out of Macalester and went to Washington, D. C, to earn money to pay for his college debts. Two years later he returned to college life—this time at the University of Minnesota—where he earned a Bachelor's Degree in political science.

During the Korean War, Mondale joined the army—mostly to get the G.I. Bill which he knew would cover most of his costs in law school. He served for two years of non-combatant duty and then entered the University of Minnesota School of Law where he earned his LLB degree in 1956.

While beginning his law practice, Walter married Joan Adams, who had been a fellow student at Macalester. Joan later became a well-known advocate of the arts, working in such institutions as the Minnesota Institute of the Arts. Before long, she was known as "Joan of Art."

In 1960, the Governor of Minnesota, Orville Freeman, for whom Mondale had worked during his election campaign, appointed him Attorney General of the State. This was his first political post of significance. Henceforth, he devoted most of his professional life to Democratic Party politics and government service.

III

One of the significant powers of the governor, in those days, was to appoint U. S. Senators when a sitting senator from his State left that office during his term. So it was that, in 1964, when Hubert Humphrey resigned from his Senate seat to become Lyndon Johnson's running mate, Freeman appointed Mondale as his replacement. He was chosen over several very prominent men mostly because of his "liberal" ideas.

In 1966, Mondale was elected to the Senate in his own right. He won again in 1972. While a senator, Walter established himself as a moderate liberal. He consistently favored all manner of civil rights for both African-Americans and women, especially in housing and employment. Foreign policy did not much interest him although he strongly opposed the war in Vietnam. In his view, foreign affairs were the prerogative of the executive branch and not Congress.

Generally pragmatic and non-confrontational, his failure to be aggressively and consistently "liberal" displeased many in his party. Once, while he was recovering from surgery to remove his appendix, one such leftist Democrat remarked: "I hope the surgeon inserted some guts before sewing him up."

The event most damaging to Mondale's reputation while he served in the Senate concerned the explosion of the space ship Apollo in 1967. This was a highly publicized disaster in which astronaut Gus Grissom and his two colleagues were killed when the spaceship exploded during a test flight. During the investigation by the Senate Committee on Aeronautic and Space Science, NASA (The National Aeronautics and Space Administration) he was exonerated from all responsibility. Most of the general public seemed to agree with the decision.

Mondale, however, wrote a minority opinion in which he criticized NASA for "evasiveness …lack of candor …patronizing …refusing to respond fully and forthrightly to …sensitivities at a time of national tragedy."

(Much later in his life, in 2001, Mondale told a reporter that his criticism had been instrumental in causing the complete restructuring of NASA and the improvement of the space program.)

IV

In 1976, President Jimmy Carter interviewed four leading Senators of the day in an effort to find a suitable running mate: Muskie of Maine, Jackson of Washington, Church of Idaho and Mondale of Minnesota. His stated intention was to find a partner in the vice president, someone capable of sharing all presidential responsibilities and, indeed, to being president himself. He chose Mondale.

During the ensuing campaign, the first televised debate between vice presidential candidates was viewed by a national audience. The debate pitted Mondale against Republican Senator Robert Dole of Kansas. Although Dole was generally regarded as having won the debate "on points" by his superior knowledge of the issues, Mondale was perceived as looking and acting more presidential and so was thought by most viewers to have been the winner.

True to his word, once elected Carter made full use of his vice president, making him privy to and seeking his opinions about all major decisions before they were made even concerning whom he was considering for major appointments in the government. Mondale also had weekly private meetings with the president and attended cabinet meetings as well as most other important meetings, including those held by national security officials.

Carter even went so far as to suggest that he and Mondale share a single staff, thereby assuring almost total integration of the two offices. This was an offer which Mondale wisely declined. This is not to say that Carter always took Mondale's advice. The president was, in most respects, more conservative than Mondale, especially on matters concerning civil rights and social welfare programs.

In the election of 1980, the pair took a drubbing from Republicans Ronald Reagan and George W. Bush. Mondale had no intention, however of giving up his true ambition which was to win the Oval Office for himself.

V

Choosing the first woman ever to seek the vice presidency, Geraldine Ferraro of New York, as his running mate, Mondale made his bid for the presidency in 1984. Running again against the ever-popular Ronald Reagan, he hurt his image badly during his Democratic Nominating Convention acceptance speech when he made a characteristically honest and straight-forward, but very unwise proclamation:

> If you elect me, I'll raise your taxes. So will Mr. Reagan. He won't tell you; but I just did.

At a time when the voting public was especially wary of increasing taxes, Mondale lost to Reagan by one of the largest margins in history: 533-13 in the Electoral College while losing nearly 60% of the popular vote.

After this loss, Mondale returned to his law practice in Minnesota. His final public office came in 1993 when President William Clinton, a fellow Democrat, appointed him Ambassador to Japan where he served with distinction until 1997.

During recent years, Mondale has been on the boards of many organizations, including the Mayo Foundation, the RAND Corporation and the University of Minnesota Foundation. He also established the Mondale Policy Forum for exploring important national issues. In his spare time, Walter enjoys reading—especially literary classics—fishing, tennis and skiing. The only significant permanent memorial to him thus far is Walter Mondale Hall, the main building on the campus of the University of Minnesota Law School. Doubtless there will be other such memorials in the future.

J. DANFORTH QUAYLE
(Courtesy of the Dan Quayle Center and Museum)

JAMES DANFORTH QUAYLE
(1947–)
1989-1993
Master of the Faux Pas

I

DESPITE A GENERALLY GOOD record as a congressman and vice president, James Danforth ("Dan") Quayle's reputation has been spoiled by a series of outlandish verbal mistakes made during public appearances. Again and again he would appear so inept that many came to regard him not only as foolish but as intellectually inferior and even incompetent.

Typical of these occurrences was the long-remembered "potatoe" incident which occurred when Quayle visited an elementary school classroom and witnessed a spelling bee. When a young boy wrote the word "potato" on the blackboard, Quayle arose from his seat in the back of the room, walked to the blackboard and changed the spelling to "potatoe." Before long a delighted press had spread news of his mistake throughout the country.

Our forty-fourth vice president was one of the youngest ever to hold that office when elected in 1989 at the age of forty-one. (Only Dwight Eisenhower and Richard Nixon had been younger.) A conservative Republican favoring limited government, Quayle was an aggressive politician for most of his career pressing for such actions as outlawing of abortion and requiring prayer in public schools. At the same time, as we shall see, he was capable of striking compromise "deals" with liberal Democrats when this suited his own agenda.

II

Dan Quayle was born in Huntington, Indiana on February 9, 1947. His father, James Quayle, managed a local newspaper and later owned papers of his own. He was a political conservative whose ideas are exemplified by his membership in the John Birch Society. He was the major influence on his son Dan's developing values. The Quayles were a wealthy family and so Dan grew up in fine houses, was introduced to the country-club lifestyle and generally enjoyed all of the advantages which wealth and high social standing usually afford.

In 1965, Quayle earned his bachelor's degree from DePauw University in political science. He then entered Indiana University School of Law but, at about the same time, joined the Indiana National Guard where he served on a part-time basis while still in school. Later, it was widely reputed that he joined the Guard only to avoid being drafted into the Army during the Vietnam War. If true, he was but one of many young men at the time who joined Guard units for just that reason. Even so, this accusation would later hurt his reputation as he sought to advance his career in public life.

While in law school, Quayle married fellow student, Marilyn Tucker. The couple jointly opened a law practice in Huntington in 1974. Marilyn shared not only his interest in law but, more importantly, his passion for politics and attainment of high office in government.

III

In 1976, with Marilyn at his side as a very effective campaign manager, Dan ran for and won a seat in the U.S. House of Representatives. He was only twenty-nine years old at the time and ran for office as an ultra conservative Republican, opposing spending for social welfare and environmental protection. He was reelected in 1978. Two years later, he won a seat in the Senate and did so again in 1986. In all of his impressive election victories he was aided immeasurably by the political skills of Marilyn.

As a senator, Quayle was effective in working out compromises with less conservative members on difficult issues, whether these concerned foreign policy toward Israel—a country which he usually did not support—or such domestic issues as government spending to assist the national economy which he also disliked. Not available for compromise, however, was his strong stand against abortion and his advocacy of prayer in public schools.

Usually, Quayle's apparently "liberal" tendencies were actually exercises in self-interest as, for example, his close collaboration with Democratic Senator, Edward Kennedy. The result of this cooperation was the Quayle-Kennedy Training for Jobs bill in 1983. This served Quayle's political interest by making him a hero in his economically depressed home State of Indiana.

IV

In 1988, Quayle began to express a strong interest in running for the vice- presidency. Republican presidential candidate, George H. W. Bush, readily agreed because he wanted a conservative as a running mate. The ensuing general election pitted the pair against Democrats, Michael Dukakis and Lloyd Bentson. It was, at times, a nasty contest with Bentson, accusing Quayle of all manner of misbehavior, most notably, his alleged draft-dodging during the Vietnam War. He was also described as being too inexperienced and not sufficiently informed or even intelligent enough for such high office.

Even so, the Bush-Quayle ticket easily defeated Dukakis and Bentson with 53% of the popular vote and 426 votes in the Electoral College.

Once in office, Bush made very little use of his vice president. Quayle was certainly not invited to share in presidential power as had been his predecessor, Walter Mondale. He was used by Bush, however, as his principal liaison with Congress, a role which Quayle performed well and with loyalty to his superior, even when he disagreed with Bush, as he often did.

The three areas in which Quayle was most active as vice president were:

1. space exploration—he chaired the National Space Council;

2. reduction of government spending and regulation, especially of state and local governments—he chaired the National Council on Competitiveness ;

3. spokesperson abroad for U. S. foreign policy—he was a member of the National Security Council and made nearly fifty visits abroad to explain and defend foreign policies.

The Bush-Quayle ticket ran for reelection in 1992 but lost this time to William Clinton and Al Gore. Their loss has been generally attributed to the poor state of the economy at the time, for which Bush's policies were blamed. Certainly Quayle's performance on the campaign trail did not help their cause. He was soon accused openly by many in the electorate of incompetence, foolishness and ignorance in matters of importance.

Among his many faux pas on the campaign trail was the aforementioned "potatoe" incident when he substituted his own incorrect spelling for the correct spelling of an elementary school student. There were many such mistakes which eventually harmed his reputation seriously. Here are a few of them:

"The Holocaust was an obscene period in our nation's history. ... No, not in our nation's but in World War II. I mean—we all lived in this century. I didn't live in this century, but in this century's history."

"I have made no good judgments. I have made good judgments in the future."

"What a waste it is to lose one's mind and not to have a mind is very wasteful."

In one of his public faux pas, Quayle created a major uproar. This was when he criticized single mothers by saying that when they defended their status they were "mocking the importance of fathers by bearing a child alone and calling it just another life-style choice." This widely circulated comment created a firestorm of protest, especially from feminists. One of them, Tanya Tucker, asked, in anger: "Who the hell is Daniel Quayle to come after single mothers?"

V

After his election defeat in 1992, Quayle returned to Indiana where he joined the conservative Hudson Institute, continued service on the Competitive Council and served on many boards of trustees. He suffered ill health from a blood clot beginning in 1995 and has led a quiet life since then. He has, however, announced that he is still available if anyone wants him to return to public life.

So far as I know, no one has yet said they wanted him to do that.

ALBERT A. GORE, JR.
(Office of the Vice President)

ALFRED "AL" GORE
(1948–)
1993-2001
The Winner Who Lost

I

ALFRED GORE, OUR FORTY-FIFTH vice president, is probably best remembered for having won the popular election for president and arguably, the Electoral College vote as well and yet, in good health and eager to take office, he never served as president. We will examine this incredible event shortly.

"Al" Gore, as he is popular known, served in Congress for sixteen years, eight years each in the House and Senate. In his long congressional career, as well as his two terms as vice president, he became one of the most assertive and successful leaders in recent history. He was—and is—famous throughout the world for his leadership in calling attention to serious environmental issues, especially the consequences of global warming. He has offered solutions to prevent or at least slow down this rapidly expanding global disaster. In 2007, he was awarded the Nobel Peace Prize for his work in this area, which included writing books and articles, giving countless speeches and traveling around much of the world to spread the word.

In addition to his work on environmental issues, Gore has, throughout his career, served on many corporate boards, been a visiting professor at several prestigious universities and provided leadership in resolving a number of critical foreign policy issues. With it all, he has been one of the most visible, influential and effective American leaders in recent years.

II

Born on March 31, 1948 in Carthage, Tennessee, Al Gore was from, his earliest years, drawn to an interest in government and politics. This was due largely to his father, Albert Gore, Sr., who was a long-time congressman, serving in the House and Senate for over thirty-two years from 1939 to 1971. Al's mother, Pauline LaFon Gore, was also a politically active parent. She was an attorney with her degree from Vanderbilt University Law School—one of its first women graduates.

At the age of nine, Al was sent to attend the prestigious St. Albans School for Boys in Washington, D.C. In 1965, he entered Harvard University where he majored in government and politics and was active in student government. At this time, his father began earnestly to encourage a career in politics for him. But after graduation in 1969 Gore enlisted in the army. He did so primarily because he had been a war protester while at Harvard and did not want this to harm his reputation—as a similar act by his father had done to himself during the Korean War.

Shortly after leaving college, Gore married Mary "Tipper" Aitcheson. The couple had four children—one boy and three girls—and remained married for forty years. They "separated amicably" in 2010.

In 1971, Gore, recently married, entered Vanderbilt Divinity School to explore the possibility of a career in religious service. He did this on a part-time basis while working as a reporter for the *Tennessean*, an important newspaper in the area. Three years later, he transferred to Vanderbilt Law School but withdrew from there as well in 1976. This time it was not because he was indecisive about his future but in order to run for a seat in the U. S. House of Representatives. Apparently, he had made up his mind at last as to the career he would pursue.

III

Given his family heritage of involvement in national politics and the useful contacts which that afforded, as well as his own interest in politics during his early years, it is not surprising that Gore won his first bid for high office. He took the seat in the House which his father had held many years before. During his eight years in this seat, he stressed the importance of recognizing the growing and dangerous impact of various forms of environmental pollution. He was also interested in public health issues generally, as well as in the threat posed by the nuclear arms race with Russia. These were areas of concern upon which he would focus for the rest of his long career in congress and the vice presidency.

Generally regarded as a "moderate," probably because, despite his generally "liberal" ideas and positions on matters of foreign and domestic policy, in the area of highly controversial issues concerning the relationship between government and personal behavior, he tended to be conservative. This was especially so in his strong and highly vocal opposition of government financed abortion and his advocacy of prayer in public schools. Similarly. he strongly opposed any sort of "gay rights."

IV

In 1988, Gore ran for the presidency. In the Democratic primary, his rivals were a distinguished group: Joe Biden, Gary Hart, Dick Gephardt, Paul Simon, Jesse Jackson and Michael Dukakis. The nomination went to Dukakis with Gore finishing in third place. The general election was won by Republican George Bush.

Four years later, when William "Bill" Clinton was nominated for the presidency on the Democratic ticket, he chose Gore as his running mate. The two were similar in so many ways: the same age, active members of the Southern Baptist Church and in agreement on most policy issues. One aspect in which they differed was their family relationships, one a notorious sexual philanderer and the other a loyal "family man" close always to his wife and children.

With it all, Gore was a popular choice with most Party leaders. A notable exception was Jesse Jackson who famously remarked at the time: "It takes two wings to fly but here you have two with the same wing." The pair won the election handily with 43% to 38% of the popular vote.

V

As vice president, Gore played an active role, assisting Clinton in most of his presidential responsibilities. Al's special interest continued to be in environmental issues, especially problems of pollution and their remedies. He launched the GLOBE program in 1994, designed to increase public awareness, especially among children. He was also involved actively in several areas of foreign policy, especially in developing early responses to Iraqi dictator Saddam Hussein's threat to American oil supplies. When Iraq invaded Kuwait and threatened Saudi Arabia, a coalition of international forces, lead by the United States, bombed Iraq and fielded a ground attack which crushed the Iraqi army.

Another foreign policy area in which Clinton delegated major responsibility to his vice president involved our relations with Latin American countries, especially Mexico. Gore played the primary role in developing and gaining approval for NAFTA (The North American Free Trade Agreement) which opened up free trade with Mexico.

Gore was also active, as vice president, in the domestic policy arena. His important study of all departments in the federal government resulted in comprehensive recommendations designed to "reinvent government." The study was conducted all over the country with political and governmental leaders actively involved. Not much came from this monumental effort, however, largely because Clinton was, by this time, becoming an increasingly unpopular president both with many of his colleagues and the general public.

Despite Clinton's declining reputation, he and Gore easily won reelection in 1996 owing largely to the lack-luster performance of their Republican opponents during the campaign. In his second term, Gore's image began to decline over issues regarding his solicitation and expenditure of campaign funds during the election and years earlier, when he was running for Governor of Tennessee.

In 1977, Gore's defense of these actions was viewed nationally on television and was seen by many as inconclusive at best and deceptive at worst. He seemed to be hiding something. In this same year, Gore compounded his problems when he visited Premier Li Ping in China, the man who had ordered the infamous massacre at Tiananmen Square in 1989. Once again, television cameras gave the event a huge audience as Gore was seen happily and warmly enjoying Li Ping's company.

Then came a final blow to Gore's reputation caused by his loyalty to a president caught up in one of the worst presidential scandals in history. This involved revelations of Clinton's history of extramarital sexual affairs while residing in the White House, especially with Monica Lewinski, a young White House intern. At the same time, there were revelations of earlier affairs with Paula Jones while he was Governor of Arkansas. These two women, Paula and Monica, became household names throughout the country as Clinton's reputation plummeted. As a result, Clinton was impeached by the House of Representatives for lying under oath while testifying in response to the allegations. He was, however, not convicted by the Senate and so remained in office.

In the midst of it all, Gore failed to distance himself from the president. To the contrary, he was an outspoken defender of Clinton, describing him in one widely distributed accolade as "one of our greatest president." This was perhaps an expression of loyalty on Gore's part but it was both unnecessary and politically damaging to him beyond anything he probably imagined at the time.

VI

Gore ran for the presidency again in 2000—this time winning the popular vote and probably the Electoral College vote as well—both narrowly. Nevertheless, he did not become president. This was the only such occurrence in our history and it happened in the following manner.

Opposing Gore in the Democratic primary was William Bradley, a former Senator from New Jersey who enjoyed widespread popularity among Democratic Party voters. Gore selected as his running mate Senator Joseph Lieberman of Connecticut, an Orthodox Jew. During the campaign against George Bush and Robert Dole, Gore did not perform well, often appearing stiff and unresponsive. He also did rather poorly in television debates with Bush.

The election was very close, finally depending on the Electoral College votes in Florida. For a time Gore seemed to be losing the contest and so he called Bush on the phone and conceded. As a recount of the vote continued, it seemed possible that he might win after all and so he called again and told Bush he was not conceding.

As television cameras watched the recount of popular and electoral votes, Florida seemed at the end to give Gore the victory, largely because of a recount of earlier contested ballots. At this point, Bush and his aides appealed to the U.S. Supreme Court to order that the recount be ended on the grounds that the date had passed by which such a recount was allowed. Therefore, they argued, the earlier count that had made Bush the winner should be verified.

The five-four decision by the Supreme Court was that, when all was said and done, Gore had lost the election in the Electoral College by four votes: 271-266. So it was that even though he had won the popular election by over a half-million votes and would have won in the Electoral College vote had the Court allowed a continuation of the vote counting, Gore was declared the loser and Bush the winner. For the first time in our history, the Supreme Court and not the electorate had decided who would hold the highest office in the land.

Following this debacle which Gore accepted in good grace, he was awarded the Nobel Peace Prize for his work on environmental issues. He has also taught at several universities, starred in a movie entitled *An Inconvenient Truth,* which received an Academy Award in 2006, and published a book the following year the title of which captures his major interest in public life: *An Inconvenient Truth: The Planetary Emergency of Global Warming and What We Can Do About It.*

From time to time, this important American still appears at public events to the delight of most who witness that he is still a highly relevant, well-informed and articulate national figure.

RICHARD B. CHENEY
(©AFP/CORBIS)

RICHARD "DICK" CHENEY
(1941–)
2001-2008
A Man of Many Parts

I

OUR FORTY-SIXTH VICE PRESIDENT, Richard Cheney, was without doubt one of the most talented, experienced and powerful figures ever to hold that office. He has been variously regarded as duplicitous and even immoral while, at the same time, one of the most important vice presidents in our history. As recently as March 6, 2013, the *New York Times* columnist, Maureen Dowd, called him "America's most powerful and destructive vice president ...a misguided power-monger who, in a paranoid spasm, led this nation into an unthinkable calamity"—the invasion of Iraq.

In addition to his two terms as vice president, Cheney was a leading American businessman who served five terms in Congress and was Secretary of Defense during an especially difficult era in American foreign policy. He was the one largely responsible for planning and executing relations with Iraq, throughout the Middle East and with the Soviet Union in the final years of the twentieth century and the early twenty-first century. His policies often involved military action.

So powerful was Cheney as vice president that he was often referred to as the "shadow president." Virtually all matters of foreign policy were referred to him by President G. W. Bush, as well as many domestic issues. Rarely has a person been so completely the president without ever having been elected to that office.

II

Born in Lincoln, Nebraska on January 30, 1949, "Dick" Cheney, as he was generally known throughout his political career, was a descendant of William Cheney who arrived in the American colonies in the seventeenth century from England. He is also a distant cousin of two American presidents, Harry Truman and Barack Obama, through Maureen Duval, a French Huguenot who came to Maryland in the late 1600's.

Dick's father, Richard Cheney, worked in the U. S. Department of Agriculture in the field of soil conservation. His mother, Marjorie Dickey Cheney, was a softball star in the 1930's.

After attended secondary schools in Lincoln and later in Casper, Wyoming, he entered Yale University but flunked out on two separate occasions. He then went to the University of Wyoming and earned his BA and MA degrees in political science. Shortly thereafter, in 1962 and again 1963, he was convicted of driving while under the influence of alcohol.

Cheney married his long-time girlfriend, Lynne Vincent in 1964. They had known each other as school classmates since he was fourteen. Lynne went on to have a highly visible and important public career in her own right, serving, for example, as Chair of the National Endowment for the Humanities from 1986-1996. The couple has two children.

During the period of the Vietnam War, Cheney began to exhibit the sort of behavior that would later lead to widespread disapproval. On five separate occasions, he eagerly sought and was granted draft deferment. When questioned about this years later, he replied in a statement which would anger many—especially servicemen and their families and friends. He said, "I had other priorities ...than military service."

III

Cheney's national political career began in 1969, during the Nixon administration, when he became an intern for Congressman William Steiger of Wyoming. He became respected for his abilities to such a degree that he soon went on to hold a number of posts in which he worked quite directly with the president and his staff. These included Deputy Assistant to the President under Nixon and Assistant to the President and White House Chief of Staff under President Gerald Ford. He was also the general campaign manager during Ford's unsuccessful bid for reelection in 1976.

In 1978, Cheney was elected to the first of five consecutive terms in Congress: 1978-1989. While in congress, he opposed the creation of a U. S. Department of Education and was a strong foe of the Head Start program designed to help poor urban children. He also opposed the involvement of Congress in any efforts to gain the release from prison by the Union of South Africa of the revolutionary hero, Nelson Mandela. He justified this widely unpopular stance by asserting that Mandela's revolutionary party, the African National Congress (ANC) was in reality a terrorist group with strong anti-American sentiments.

Shortly after George H. W. Bush became president in 1989, he appointed Cheney his Secretary of Defense. He held this post for about four years. His long-standing reputation as a forceful, decisive and effective leader stems in large measure from his performance as Secretary of Defense. The first important example of his "take-charge" approach to foreign policy was the military action in Panama in 1989 to oust dictator Manuel Noriega. Cheney personally directed the entire operation which resulted in Noriega's capture and imprisonment.

A more significant venture for Cheney was military action in the Middle East. This would involve a long conflict for control of Kuwait, a small oil-rich country which Iraq claimed and then took by force in 1990. Saddam Hussein, the Iraqi dictator was threatening to attack Saudi Arabia, our closest ally in the region. Cheney travelled to that country and convinced its leadership to allow thousands of American troops to fight from there against Iraq—along with soldiers from European countries, including England, France and Germany.

Thus began what came to be known as "Operation Desert Storm." The result was largely successful despite much criticism for what many regarded as our too early withdrawal from Iraq which allowed Hussein to remain in power. Generally speaking, however, Cheney's reputation around the world rose to new heights because of the key role he played in this long and complex conflict. At the very least, oil supplies to the West were resumed, Iraq was tamed and a degree of peace returned to the Middle East—at least for a while.

A few years later, late in 1992, Democrat William Clinton assumed the presidency and Cheney retired from national politics and moved to Dallas, Texas where he soon became CEO of the Halliburton Company which supplies construction and technical services to the oil industry world-wide. He held this post from 1995-2000. Once again, however, despite a generally successful performance as a business leader, he became involved in a scandal which later would harm his political career.

When being questioned by a Congressional committee about his suitability to serve as vice president, he was asked about his personal wealth which at the time was estimated to be nearly $100 million. The committee was particularly interested to know whether his wealth was derived from illegal decisions made while he was CEO at Halliburton. Specifically, had he known about—or, perhaps even ordered—the illegal sale of company stock to another company at a purposely inflated price, resulting in unusually high returns for Halliburton executives?

In the event, Cheney was never convicted of wrong doing. He did, however, leave Halliburton in 2000 with a $20 million severance payment.

IV

Despite this scandal, George W. Bush chose Cheney as his running mate in 2000. The pair won the election but remained purposely apart for the first year or so of their term. There had been threats to their lives attributed to Iraqi terrorists and so it seemed best if they were not together in case the president was killed. Cheney stayed in an undisclosed location and was heavily guarded.

Following the "9/11" attack on the World Trade Center in New York, Cheney pushed for a renewed war against Iraq and planned what became known as the "War on Terror." He claimed that Saddam Hussein was responsible for the attack even though U.S. intelligence agencies said there was no "credible evidence" that he was involved. Cheney had little success in convincing the public that war was necessary. Public opinion polls showed that most Americans opposed another war with Iraq. When told on ABC News that there would likely be very little support, his response was:

SO?

Much criticism followed this response throughout the country.

Bush and Cheney were elected for a second term in 2004. It was during the campaign against Democrats John Kerry and John Edwards that a more personal scandal adversely affected Cheney. This involved public revelation of his daughter Mary's lesbianism. His response was that he personally favored gay marriage but that the legality of it should be left to the determination of state and local governments and not be resolved at the federal level.

During his second term as vice president, there was a much larger scandal. This one involved alleged CIA "leaks" to the press of confidential reports on Iraq's military weaponry while he was Secretary of Defense. His chief of staff at the time, Lewis "Scooter" Libby, testified that they had both personally approved the leak. In the event, Libby was convicted of treason but Cheney was released. After failing to gain a presidential pardon for Libby, Cheney described him as being just like any "soldier on a battle field."

Toward the close of his vice presidency in June, 2007, a long article about Cheney in the *Washington Post* summed up the extent of his power and influence while in office by saying that, in many ways, he and not Bush had been the real president.

V

In retirement, Cheney has enjoyed several sumptuous homes in Virginia, Wyoming and Maryland. He has remained politically quite vocal, mostly with criticisms of President Obama. He has been especially critical of the new president's foreign and national security policies. For example, in December, 2009, just after an attempted bombing of a passenger airplane, he said : We "are at war when President Obama pretends we aren't ..." A year later, on an ABC television program, he charged that Obama was wrongly branding "terrorist attacks as criminal acts as opposed to acts of war," which, he said, they truly were.

Finally, he did praise the president for something. This was the operation which resulted in the killing of Osama bin Laden. Apparently, what Cheney liked best was any strong and even violent action which led to clear and definitive results. No great admirer of Obama-style compromise and accommodation was he! Perhaps this is part of the reason why he had only a 30% approval rating in a recent national public opinion poll, compared with a 60% rating about a decade ago.

In 2011, Cheney completed his personal memoir: *In My Time: A Personal and Political Memoir.* This is an often self-serving account of his accomplishments. A heavy smoker for most of his adult life—two to three packages of cigarettes daily—Cheney suffered four severe heart attacks between 1984 and 2010. In 2012, he had a heart transplant. At the time of this writing, April, 2013 he is seventy-one years old and living an uncharacteristically quiet life.

Joe Biden

47th Vice President of the United States

JOSEPH BIDEN
(1942–)
(2008–)
Still Going Strong

I

BIOGRAPHERS—A CAREFUL LOT—RARELY WRITE about people who are still alive, much less still in the midst of their careers. This way the author runs little risk of being criticized by his subject for inaccuracies or misrepresentations. Nevertheless, I have decided to offer at least a partial account of the life and career of our sitting vice president who is now in the early stage of his second term. By so doing, I can bring this account up to date as of the time of this writing.

Joseph Biden was elected to seven consecutive terms in the U. S. Senate and was twice an unsuccessful presidential candidate before his first run for the vice presidency in 2008. He was the first Roman Catholic to serve as vice president. Like his predecessor, Dick Cheney, he was both praised and criticized for his record in public life. The criticism was largely focused on what many regarded as his rambling, long-winded speeches and for the persistent errors and gaffes in them.

II

Joseph "Joe" Biden was born on November 20, 1942 in Scranton, Pennsylvania. His father, Joseph, was a rather poor man at the time of Joe's birth during an economic depression in Scranton. In 1956, the family moved to Claremont, Delaware and later to Wilmington where his father was a used-car salesman and the family living standard rose slightly.

After attending Achmere Academy in Claremont, Biden enrolled at the University of Delaware where he excelled at sports and social life but did rather poorly in his studies, graduating in 1965 with an AB degree in political science. He ranked 506th in a class of 688. Entering Syracuse University College of Law in 1965, he found studies to be "the biggest bore in the world" but managed to earn his law degree in 1968, ranking 27th in a class of 85. While in law school, he was accused of plagiarizing and received a grade of "F" in that class.

In 1966, while still in law school, Biden married Nelia Hunter, whom he had met while a student at the University of Delaware. The couple has three children: Joseph, Robert and Maria. At about this time, Biden sought and received five draft deferments during the Vietnam War—very like a number of his predecessors during other wars.

During his early years as a law student and attorney, Joe was active in local politics as a member of the Republican Party but he came to dislike President Nixon so intensely that he switched to the Democratic Party in 1969. After being elected in that same year to the New Castle Delaware County Council by a huge majority in a solidly Republican district, he began to have serious thoughts about running for national office.

III

Biden's entry onto the national political scene came in 1972 when he made a highly improbable bid for a seat in the U. S. Senate. I say "improbable" because the Republican occupant of that seat, Caleb

Boggs, was so firmly entrenched in that position that no one wanted to run against him. In addition, Biden had no funds to undertake such a campaign.

That he won the election is owing largely to the efforts of his sister, Valerie Owens, and other members of his family who managed a very personal, door-to-door campaign. With much energy and enthusiasm, Biden and his family won the election in a major upset victory. He would go on to win this Senate seat for the next five consecutive elections—until 2008, when he resigned to run for the vice presidency.

Several weeks after his election in 1972, Biden suffered a terrible tragedy. His wife, Nelia, and baby daughter, Maria, were killed in a tragic automobile accident. Less than five years later, in 1977, he remarried. He and his new wife, Jill Jacobs have a daughter and have become very active members in the Roman Catholic Church.

Early in his first term in the Senate, in 1974, *Time Magazine* named Biden one of "200 Faces for the Future," calling him "self-confident" and "compulsively ambitious." By this time he was already gaining a national reputation for his advocacy of laws to protect the natural environment from industrial pollution as well as his support of consumer protection laws and his strong push for an arms control agreement with the Soviet Union. He met personally with Russian Foreign Minister, Andrei Gromyko, to help negotiate the Salt Arms Control Treaty of 1979.

Later in his long Senate career, Biden was active in relations with many foreign countries, notably the Union of South Africa. He was strongly opposed to the apartheid policies of that nation and urged President Ronald Reagan, in 1986, to impose harsh economic sanctions until the discrimination In South Africa against Black Africans was ended.

In 1988, Biden ran for the presidential nomination on the Democratic ticket. His opponent was Michael Dukakis. During the campaign he was accused of plagiarizing a recent speech by Neil Kinnock, the leader of the British Labour Party. He was also accused of "lifting" phrases from speeches by Robert Kennedy, John F. Kennedy and Hubert Humphrey. All of these accusations were probably true. He also lied outright—or at least greatly exaggerated—when describing his record as a student in law school. In September, 1987, he withdrew from the race, citing what he described as unfair exaggerations of his "past mistakes."

Continuing with his Senate career on into the later twentieth and early twenty-first centuries, Biden served as a key member of both the Judiciary and Foreign Relations Committees. For some years, he was chair of the Judiciary Committee and a strong proponent of civil liberties, especially for women and African Americans. He was instrumental in the passage of the *Violence Against Women Act* of 1994—commonly referred to as the "Biden Crime Law" and called this the "single most significant legislation during my 35-year tenure in the Senate."

As a member of the Senate Foreign Relations Committee, Biden was regarded as a liberal internationalist. He favored the training of Bosnian Muslims to resist oppression in Bosnia despite the fact that the U. S. presidents of the time opposed any military involvement in the Balkans. He also supported the bombing in Bosnia by NATO forces and called his role in that part of the world during the 1990s his "proudest moment in public life" related to foreign policy.

IV

Despite some strains in their relationship, Barack Obama picked Biden to be his running mate in the 2007 presidential election. He selected him primarily because of his ability as a campaigner and his appeal to ordinary citizens who tended to respond well to his warm and friendly style. The pair won the election handily against Senator John McCain and Alaska Governor, Sarah Palin: 365-173 in the Electoral College and 53%-46% of the popular vote.

As vice president, Biden served at first as a behind-the-scenes advisor to the president. He traveled to Iraq several times to deliver Obama's messages personally to that country's leaders. He also supervised the president's stimulus package to combat recession in the domestic economy. Before long, however, he began to commit the same sort of public gaffes that hurt his reputation—in much the same manner as his predecessor, Dick Cheney.

As early as 2009, he said in a public speech that the best way to avoid catching the swine flu that was spreading rapidly throughout the east coast was to avoid travel on all trains and subways. He was ordered by the White House to retract this statement but the damage had been done.

Shortly thereafter, Biden committed another gaffe when he said publically that the administration had "misread how bad the economy was." At about this time, he was overheard saying to the president, in what he mistakenly assumed to be a private conversation, that the *Patient Protection and Affordable Care Act* was "a big fucking deal." Of course, a delighted press widely distributed all of these embarrassing remarks.

Of Biden's proclivity for making such inappropriate remarks, his Senate colleague, Lindsey Graham, once said: "If there were no gaffes, there would be no Joe." Similarly, a white House advisor said of Biden: "His gaffes are what make him so endearing ... he wouldn't change him one bit."

In 2012, Obama and Biden were re-elected by a comfortable margin, this time over Republicans Mitt Romney and Paul Ryan. Shortly thereafter, an issue of the *New York Times* featured an article by Mark Lander which attributed Biden's success as vice president to his ability to develop close personal relationships with leaders throughout the world including, most importantly, Chinese Premier Xi Jinping.

National organizations which have given Biden high ratings for his first term in office include such progressive groups as the American Civil Liberal Union (ACLU), the National Education Association (NEA) and the American Federation of Labor and Congress of Industrial Organizations (AFL/CIO). Of course, it is too early to tell what the final judgment on Biden's political career will be. He might still be president. After all, he is only seventy years old.